OUR WORDS

The Social Politics of Homosexuality, Religion and Race

BY
XAVIER JAMES

Onyx Media Group

INTRODUCTION

On Valentines Day 2010 the children in an all boy's class at "Capt. Columbus" elementary school were chewing on their Valentine's Day candy. Upon seeing this-the teacher, "Mr. Watson" in a seething homosexual slur, demanded that they **"suck"** their candy; **"you can't chew in my class you have to suck. Don't chew, suck,"** he demanded. This homosexual teacher, in a public school, in charge of instructing, molding and teaching these boys how to be men, was doing the exact opposite. One can only imagine why he'd be concerned about how little boys ate their candy unless it somehow fascinated him. Or maybe watching first grade boys suck on lollipops somehow turned him on; you decide. But if **'all men teach as they do'** then his annoying gay slur, female walk and mannerisms are being recorded and processed as acceptable, respectable and normal male behavior to this group of first grade boys. What's also disturbing is that this all boy's class exchanged valentine cards intended for the opposite sex. Remember, there are no girls in their class. God knows if they go on a field trip they'd be paired off and taught to hold hands with each other. The overt and subliminal homosexual programming here is obvious. This same school also includes a all girl's class with no boys. Get the picture. A month later "Mr. Watson" told his boys to **"say that you're 'gay' whenever you're happy, because 'gay' means that you're happy. Say you're gay."** Gay hasn't meant happy in over fifty years.

This 'experiment' was designed to prove that in a classroom setting girls presented a distraction for boys and vice versa. The architects of this plan insist that separating the sexes gave each group better grades. That's debatable. Because the problem was never the children's capacity to learn, its always been the teacher's inability to teach. The sad but true fact is that most teachers gave up teaching years ago. They only show up at school everyday just to get a paycheck. And they have no problem blaming our children for not learning what they've been unsuccessful at teaching. If the goal of school is to prepare children for life how does separating them along the gender line help? In every aspect of life, girls and boys, men and women are going to interact and compete on every level. Real life is full of distractions.

The military teaches aggression. Christian schools teach Christianity. And homosexual teachers teach homosexuality; by word or deed. It's inescapable. Would you have an anti-war activist teach at a military academy? Would you let an anti-abortionist teach a class on stem cell research? No, and why not, because every truth would be blurred and every fact skewed and every viewpoint catered to fit their philosophy and agenda. Would you let a homosexual priest teach alter boys? Now that poses another question; If Christian priests can't keep their hands off little boys how can you expect a homosexual male who believes he should've been born a women, to keep his views or his hands to himself? Just like within the Catholic Church pedophiles protect other pedophiles, let's watch and see who comes to the defense of these homosexual teachers. It was no accident homosexual male was placed in charge of these boys. The principal or school board is directly responsible and they knew it would be years before any parent knows the damage that's been done to their child. What gave them the right to put your son or daughter in harms way? This is yet another homosexual strategy to introduce gullible children to same sex environments at an early and impressionable age. And weather you approve, disapprove, agree, disagree, like it or not, you and your children are part of this far reaching plan.

CONTENTS

Analysis and Solution

You know what's funny? The way people look at you when you say the word "conspiracy." They automatically assume that you're paranoid or crazy. It seems we've been programmed not believe our own eyes. When I say conspiracy, you automatically start thinking about JFK and Oswald. And more recently, 9/11 and the war on terror. Because of the shear magnitude of the acts, we'd much rather believe it was the work of a couple of nut-jobs acting alone then the carefully orchestrated schemes of seemingly rational people in high places.

But it is our feeling of helplessness that makes us ignore the obvious and pretend the evidence doesn't exist. We gladly interject doubt into our own minds because we feel powerless to stop the crime or bring its perpetrators to justice. So we go about our day pretending conspiracies don't exist and don't affect our lives. Some of us actually fear that if there is a conspiracy, we may be called upon to do something about it.

Well maybe you'd be less skittish if from here on out I use the word; **Plan**. Several individuals in positions of authority collectively made **plans** to deceive those who trusted them. A number of far reaching **plans** have been exposed over the years which validated the claims made by so called 'conspiracy theorists'. The reason why this is important is because at the time the accusations were made nobody believed them. They were called conspiracy theorists and laughed at. Eventually the truth came out and the accusers were vindicated. But the damage was already done. This book is the result of identifying and analyzing a social construct that affect the lives of everyone on this planet. Recognizing a problem is the first step in finding a solution.

<u>IN THE BEGGINING</u>

Where Did Homosexuality Originate?

Now, where did homosexuality historically originate? **Who started all the sodomizing?** That's what you really want to know, right? Well, contrary to popular belief, it wasn't in Sodom and Gomorrah as the Bible will tell you. It's started in the Caucus Mountain region where one cave man wanted to show his dominance over another. This is the ancestry by which the Greeks emerged. Although Greece proceeded what we now call Europe today, hordes of barbarians roamed throughout the region until they were supposedly 'civilized' by the Romans. The Romans adopted the Greek homosexual prototype and injected it throughout Europe. And from that point on wherever Europeans traveled around the globe, so went homosexuality.

Why is Greece so important when it comes to homosexuality? Because the ancient Greeks were the greatest perverts and pedophiles the world has ever known. They organized and institutionalized the rape and abduction of their own children. They objectified young boys to the point where it was acceptable and legal to walk up to them on the street and literally grope their genitals. Sparta and the Athens were the real Sodom and Gomorrah. They sure as hell didn't teach us that in school. In exchange for being raped, young boys received knowledge, education, philosophy, and shelter. In fact, to be a mentor to a young boy meant you weren't just his teacher, you were also the young boy's rapist. And there wasn't any escaping or running away. It was the law. And this perversion of nature lasted generation after generation after generation.

To say that Greek men loved young boys would be an understatement. Their fascination with pedophilia (as its called today) is evident in their mythology, vases, sculptures, poems, statues and even religion. Their god Zeus was a homosexual rapist. Hercules was a homosexual who had sexual relations with both males and females. We all know that a god reflects its people; so can you imagine the sick minds that fostered these types of ideas. It was the custom for a young boy between the age of twelve and sixteen to be paired with an older male between the ages of 26-30. The young boy would be wooed with gifts and flirtation, basically forced into the role nature had designated for the female. I've often wondered how a father could possibly pass his own child off to be raped; knowing what pain and confusion was in store because his own father had allowed him to be raped around that exact same age. In some cities young boys were actually abducted by the older man and taken away for two months holiday to celebrate their union. This abduction and rape was called "the honeymoon;" sound familiar?

To assure that these sexual assaults were aimed at young boys near and around puberty; older males were often teased, ridiculed or outright forbidden to be the passive partner once they reached adulthood. After years of abuse and homosexuality, they were expected to go back home and live with their wives. Although older Greek males married young females, they didn't actually live together for about 12 years. This was because their military training came first. But these males only married for reproductive purposes; love and passion was saved for the young boys. Women were excluded and forbidden education or any type of intellectual scholarship. They were considered unworthy of a man's love, respect or attention; only men and boys deserved that privilege. That's why pictures of women are rare. So it stands to reason why homosexual relationships between older women and young girls evolved and was encouraged.

The Greeks completely systematized homosexuality. Their individual needs always came first. Some Greeks would even castrate young slave boys as a way to prolong their use. To be a Greek soldier was to be homosexual. When you were on the battlefield, you weren't just fighting next to your comrade, you were fighting for and to impress your lover. Homosexuality was mandatory within the military. That's why the Greeks were such fierce fighters. When I watched the movie *"300"* I just shook my head at how Hollywood tried to convince us that Sparta was so different from the rest of Greece. It was an entertaining movie but historically incorrect. They literally tried to rewrite history. Greek writers will tell you as much. They documented so much of their perversions that it's impossible to deny. Even the first Olympics were some kind of weird, nude, exhibitionist folly. Let's tell the truth; if Socrates was Plato's mentor wasn't he also his rapist? He describes his mentor as boy crazy. Plato said Socrates 'would lose his damn mind (his senses) whenever he was in the presence of beautiful boys.' If that isn't a sick mind I don't know what is.

Yet these are the people we learn about in school. These are the greatest minds admired throughout European society…unbelievable. But we're also inundated with Roman folklore. One cannot mention Greece and not mention Rome. When it comes to perversion they're one in the same. In Rome incest ran rampant; fathers slept with their daughter and brothers with their own sisters. The Romans took homosexuality to a whole new level. They created laws and codes outlining to the smallest details the use of their homosexual practices; much like homosexuals are trying to do today. Certain types of homosexuals couldn't hold office while others could. Certain types of homosexuals couldn't join the military while others could. But lets be clear; to be a Roman soldier meant that you were 100% homosexual. I imagine they had their own 'don't ask, don't tell' military policy in place.

Many have argued that homosexuality and decadence is what led to the demise of the

Roman Empire. They didn't produce enough male soldiers or leaders to sustain their military or government. Historians tried their best to hide the wide extent of Roman homosexuality from the world. Of course that's due to <u>Histor</u>ians rewriting <u>Hi</u>story as usual. It's the same woman haters who initiated the Inquisition and the witch trials. Can you imagine a man getting tired of his wife and accusing her of being a witch just to get out of his marital duties; knowing full well his accusation would lead to her death?

The 'genderside' of European women lasted for over 400 years. Records indicate that millions of women were raped, tortured and killed for the crime of simply being a woman. The Catholic Church was especially proficient with torture devices such as the '**Breast Ripper**,' mangling and ripping women's breasts off. They also relished a hideous contraption called **'The Pair'** which was inserted into the female's vagina or rectum and upon turning, sharp pointed blades would expand while inside the woman, causing internal mutilation. By attacking the woman's breasts she would be unable to nurse a child. And by mutilating her womb she'd be unable to bear one. Is there any doubt about how much these particular homosexuals envied and hated women? Sure, someone will argue that men and children were also killed. But the particulars of the murder devices reveal a much sinister plot.

As Europeans spread across the globe so did disease and perversion. From the Caucus Mountains to Greece to Rome to Europe to the new world (America), Homosexuality, rape, sadism, sexism and greed traveled. Homosexuals, thieves, killers, rapists and pedophiles made up the bulk of colonists and Christopher Columbus' crew. They were the scourge of Europe. In fact, Columbus himself was so depraved he;

> 'Celebrated his arrival in the New World by capturing four native boys-
>   took them into his cabin to sexually abuse and sodomize them.'
>   -Baruti p. 228

The explorers' sexual imperative didn't just stop with their 'sea wives.' The term 'sea wife' refers to homosexuals aboard ships heading to far away places, behaving like man and wife while at sea. Upon arrival these same sailors would then pursue women. That is how perversion is spread. Columbus, by the way, was a devout Christian. But isn't that how it always is? Anyway, sexually repressed Puritans landed at Plymouth Rock bringing with them their most depraved practices; lies, hypocrisy, sexism, self flogging, sadomasochism and slavery. Jamestown was practically San Francisco today; complete with same sex wedding ceremonies. The European male's hatred of women is evident throughout European/American history. And any culture that hates its women will see an increase in violence towards them as well as a decrease in the family unit.

It reminds me of how the Black youth of today rap about misogyny and the degradation of their women. While other cultures sing songs in praise of their women, we are the only race on earth that sing and dance to songs of violence and humiliation towards our females. Is there any wonder why homosexuality rises as family values decline.

Anyway, America's founding father's perversions were well hidden and suppressed by the media of the time, but became woven into American society. Benjamin Franklin's drug abuse and love of prostitutes has been well documented as the cause of his syphilis. Of course the little boys' body's found buried beneath his house was somebody else's handiwork; not his. Alexander Hamilton and John Lauren's homosexual relationship was compared to their European forefathers Damon and Pythias. Then there's Lewis and Clark; Lewis preferred killing himself then to be without Clark. President Franklin Pierce and Nathaniel Hawthorne, President James Buchanan and William Rufus King, Gen. George Washington's 'buggery' was well hidden. Once again that's due to Historians rewriting History. They burned a lot of his letters and documentation to cover up his homosexuality. But old George had a secret relationship with Marquis De Lafayette and was linked to fellow homosexual founding father Alexander Hamilton. Washington had a Black slave he took everywhere and did everything with; including pose for portraits. That was very unusual for a slave master unless there was something else going on. Upon his death, the general left his now freed slave very well off.

 George Washington also had a well known pedophile, Baron Friedrich Wilhelm Von Steuben, train his army at Valley Forge. I wonder how he would have felt about today's military's "don't ask, don't tell" policy. The president obviously had no problem with pedophiles. I wonder if George Washington was around today would the Barron be training troops at fort Brag or spending quality time in Leavenworth? And don't get me started on the very angry and confused homosexual J. Edger Hoover who waged war against Blacks and poor Whites for over a quarter century. These were the founders, practitioners and protectors of homosexuality in America. Add to that the influence of the woman hating, alter boy loving religious hierarchy of the time and you see how we arrived where we are today. Western society was built on homosexuality.

What Causes Homosexual Impulses?

Since homosexuality is not hereditary or genetic what causes homosexual desires? Listed below are the **Family Research Institutes** four categories. Notice their categories will be consistent with what we will be discussing throughout this study. (*Italics mine*):

1. <u>Homosexual experience:</u>
*any homosexual experience in childhood, especially if it is a first sexual experience or with an adult- *notice how this is listed as number 1*
*any homosexual contact with an adult, particularly with a relative or authority figure

2. <u>Family abnormality:</u>
*a dominant, possessive or rejecting mother
*an absent, distant or rejecting father
*a parent with homosexual proclivities, particularly one who molests a   child of the same sex
*a sibling with homosexual tendencies, particularly one who molests a brother or sister
*divorce, which often lead s to sexual problems for both the children and the adults
*parents who model unconventional sex roles
*condoning homosexuality as a legitimate lifestyle-*allowing your children to hang out with and/or be constantly subjected to their indoctrination.*
* *the lack of spirituality within the home*

3. <u>Unusual sexual experience, particularly in early childhood</u>
* precocious or excessive masturbation
*exposure to pornography in childhood
*depersonalized sex (e.g., group sex, sex with animals)-*when you objectify the person or thing as merely a vessel for your pleasure, the sex act becomes more relevant then the person or thing, nothing becomes more important than the gratification you get from the act; and you start not to care about anything other then your immediate need to be satisfied*
*or girls, sexual interaction with adult males-*nobody tells girls or young women that their first sexual experience can be painful and down right unpleasant. Quite a few are mentally ill-prepared. They end up disappointed and psychologically traumatized altogether by the painful experience; thus more susceptible to what can be called 'alternative lifestyles'*

4. <u>Cultural influences</u>

*A visible and socially approved homosexual sub-culture that invites curiosity and encourages exploration-*MTV's homosexual programming, women being applauded for kissing each other, songs praising homosexuality and experimentation*

*pro-homosexual sex education

*openly homosexual authority figures, such as teachers- *other than the mother and father, a teacher is the most important person in a society; especially in a developing child's eyes. Good, bad or indifferent, a teachers words and deeds stays with a person their entire lives.*

*societal and legal toleration of homosexual acts-*homosexual friendly legislation*

*depictions of homosexuality as normal and/or desirable behavior-*since the mass media is controlled by homosexuals those depictions are everywhere.*

5. <u>DRUGS</u>-*makes you do all kinds of crazy s***!*

Born That Way-Or Manufactured?

"The fulfilling of sex roles via homosexuality destroys the idea that it is anything more than a chosen behavior. These *males* choosing to swap roles but still assign masculine and feminine parameters, makes the homosexual born gay idea bunk. These *males* choose their roles depending upon the moral relevance of the situation…homosexuality is a behavior that does nothing to enhance or sustain a community…*it's* simply sex without responsibility."
-Eran Reya (italics mine)

Let me break it down for you; If a male says he's born gay at what point does he choose to become the penetrated partner in his relationships? How do two males go about the business of planning which one takes on the masculine role in a relationship if they're both born to be females? At what point does a woman choose to take on the masculine role in her relationship? The power specific roles homosexuals choose within their relationships is exactly that; choice. **It is an undisputed, scientific fact that nature didn't design a man's anal cavity to be penetrated by objects; period.** That includes a penis.

According to the **American Psychiatric Association** (Fact Sheet on Sexual Orientation 2000) there is no gay gene. 'There are no replicated scientific studies supporting any specific biological etiology for homosexuality.'

The **University of Illinois** screened the entire human genome system. The study led by Dr. Brian Mustanski concluded; 'there is no gay gene.'

In 2000 an **Australian study** of identical twins found only 20% of their male homosexuals and 24% of their female homosexuals had a gay twin. Remember, identical twins have identical genes so the study should have revealed 100% that all the siblings were homosexual. But it didn't. Therefore, it substantiates that homosexuality is a socially conditioned behavior.

To date, no doctor has found one single hereditary/ genetic, physical or hormonal difference between heterosexuals and homosexuals; period. Second, *"born that way"* is a label usage, propaganda tool homosexuals engage to maintain political credibility; even tying themselves to the civil rights movement. It is a psychological ploy used to secure homosexual friendly legislation that fits their agenda. It's disgusting to hear homosexuals equate Black oppression with a perverted sex-style. But the question was; can a person be born homosexual? Absolutely not! But that's like asking can a person be born retarded. There will always be exceptions to any rule. We'll discuss that later. But for now pay close attention. The number one cause of male homosexuality is pedophilia! Every single study, statistic, questionnaire or survey gives the same consistently indisputable data; older, homosexual males molesting and raping young boys creates the trauma that leads to the mental disorder called homosexuality. Let me reiterate. What turns a man homosexual? A few things are culprit; however, the number one catalyst is trauma by rape. No one is "born that way." They are turned that way either as innocent children, unsuspecting adolescents or curious adults.

In a 1992 study, sex researchers K. Freud and R.I. Watson published findings in the Journal of Sex and Marital Therapy revealing that homosexual males are three times more likely than straight men to engage in pedophilia, and that the average pedophile victimizes between 20 and 150 boys before being arrested.

One must seriously examine and analyze the long term emotional effects rape has on a child; especially a male child. Since most rapes are not reported to authorities and little children rarely tell their parents about sexual abuse, a boy who's been molested will usually internalize his fears, anger and helplessness. His mind will constantly play back the trauma of being held down, bent over and viciously penetrated. Since most children are sexually assaulted by someone they know and in a lot of cases trusts, child victims will seldom tell on an abusive uncle, stepfather, cousin, neighbor or family friend. They think other adults won't believe the allegation and/or would be powerless to protect them.

In the meantime this young child will continue living and aging with this horrible experience inside of him. And bare in mind that most child rapist continue to rape their young victim for years or until circumstance prevents them from having contact with that child. Child victims often do not develop naturally without some form of counseling, therapy or support. If women who are raped can suffer Post Traumatic Stress Syndrome
then imagine the fate of little boys.

Young victims who blame themselves for being raped often fall into one of two categories; *One*, they become angry, overly aggressive, extremely distrustful; see a collapse in relationships with family and friends. And in an attempt to offset the physical feeling of helplessness left by the rapist, they themselves become physically and emotionally predatory on some level, towards others. Or *secondly*, they become quiet, withdrawn, passive, see a collapse in relationships with family and friends, become callously self destructive and very compliant to the will of others.

The most common self destructive behaviors among sexual assault victims are drugs, alcohol, prostitution and sex. Since most victims of sexual abuse follow similar behavioral patterns child victims can also become less interested in school, socializing and sports. Watch the signs. Pedophiles completely destroy children. Their innocence is snatched away and replaced with physical trauma and emotional scarring. They suddenly experience emotions, ideas and thoughts that only mature adults can deal with.

Although a child knows that a pedophile touching them is wrong, often the feelings and sensations they're experiencing creates the inner conflict. 'Its wrong, but it feels good physically.' The immediate shame of deriving pleasure from a sexual assault is lingering and psychologically damaging. Think about this: can a woman derive pleasure from being raped? Does she hate herself for having an orgasm while some animal has a knife to her throat? That's part of the guilt and shame that prevents rape victims from not telling on their predator. Although a horrible scenario the trauma of sexual assault is far reaching and completely life altering.

Data continues to show that there is a very strong relationship between a male being sodomized as a child and his seeking to do the same to other children once he becomes an adult…..the younger the age at which homosexual rape (or molestation) occurs, and the more traumatic the abuse, the greater the likelihood that it will be a confusing influence in the individuals sexual orientation. (Baruti 67-68)

According to the U.S. department of Justice (child victimizers pg 7) about 95% of child victimizers and 86% of adult victimizers who reported having been abused physically or sexually said that such abuse had occurred while they were children….among those who suffered physical or sexual abuse before age 18, 36% had child victims, among those who suffered abuse after entering adulthood, 13% had child victims. ( )

As the young male victim of a homosexual rapist/pedophile gets older, without psychological help his developmental disorder festers. He will not only fall into one of the two categories discussed early on, but he will often develop an inability to connect with the opposite sex. He will; a) identify with his abusers homosexuality or b) abuse woman physically or emotionally. Either way the natural, development of the male to female bond never grows and advances. His untreated trauma and long held feelings of distrust and powerlessness will someday cause him to use his penis as a weapon against others and/or to surrender his own anus.

A 1988 study of 229 convicted child molesters published in the **Archives of Sexual**

Behavior found that 86% of Pedophiles described themselves as homosexual or Bi-sexual. **Alfred Kinsey** found in 1948 that 37% of all male homosexuals admitted to having sex with children less than 17 years of age. Also in the **Archives of Sexual behavior,** a 2000 study revealed 39 out of 48 homosexual males preferred having sexual relations with fifteen and twenty year old males, and as many as 40% of males who are attracted to children prefer boys.

In a homosexual magazine called 'The Advocate' Carl Maves said " how many gay men, I wonder, would have missed out on a valuable, liberating experience-one that would have initiated them into their sexuality-if it weren't for so called molestation."

The frankness in such a statement is frightening. The sickness of the publishers to print such perversion is telling. The statement motivates and rationalizes the rape of our young and feeds the magazines readership its much needed confirmation in committing heinous acts against children. I wonder how many children Maves himself has "liberated?" Homosexual activists around the world work tirelessly to lower the legal age of consent and overturn any sodomy laws they haven't already changed. I'm not saying that all homosexuals are fixated with children, but studies show a very uneven number are. Homosexuals as a distinct group are over represented in child molestation cases when compared with heterosexuals. I can't count how many times I've heard homosexuals say they were introduced to homosexuality at a very young age by an older, predatory male figure.

If you're the parent of a homosexual son or daughter go talk to them or other relatives. You need to find out who your child interacted with when they were young; because it's highly probable your child's homosexuality is the result of childhood molestation or rape. And that definitely was not their choice! God is not gender confused; in fact the creator is very gender specific. It's why men have the outer strength and women have the inner strength. It's why men are hunter gatherers and women are protector nurturers.
Born that way, not likely, turned that way; probable. Rape can be connected to the promiscuity in some men and the collapse of moral values in a lot of women. That's why psychological trauma is the ultimate game changer.

Why are so many women turning homosexual?

There is no one cause we can point to as the catalyst for the recent lesbian explosion. But there are five prevailing factors that must be addressed and we will now discuss as reasons A, B, C, D and E. In case you haven't noticed, as regard for men and respect for fathers decreases, homosexuality in women increases. As the very meaning of the word 'man' is constantly taking a beating, the meaning of the word 'woman' has mutated into variations of its original concept. Enter feminism.

A.) Feminism

Feminism: n. 1. Belief in the social, political and economic equality of the sexes. 2.

The movement organized around this belief.

The primary strategy of the <u>feminist</u> movement is to make women seem physically, mentally and emotionally stronger then men. Feminists create and facilitate images of men as weak, incapable, non-thinking brutes. Careful emphasis is placed on a man's lack of sensitivity-----Women who are placed in positions of authority now more than ever politicize these positions. They constantly display an overt disrespect of the male role at work and in the home. In countless cases it simply boils down to if a man has to eat, he has to in some way rely on the woman. He must rely on a woman at home who earns more money then him before going to work and take orders from a woman who also earns more then him. In the past ten years alone, the prototype of the man as the primary provider has systematically been eroded.

Women now dominate the workforce; strategically placed in charge of men in all areas of the workplace. Instead of creating an atmosphere of equality European business owners are now propping up women in power positions once held by men; still maintaining an imbalance and still creating an unbalanced power structure.

What was the chasm that made feminism necessary? For European women, feminism was essential to combat centuries of European male abuse, misogyny, and outright disdain. Initially, feminism was allowed by European men to give their women the illusion of power, in exchange they wanted peace and quiet at the dinner table. You see, European men since they've existed have subjugated their women. European women lived in constant fear of European men. Their first model societies were full of arrogant males who decided females weren't intelligent enough to teach or respect. Greek and Roman societies, which Americans hold in such high esteem, actually, to a large degree, hated their women but loved the little boys. In pedophile societies like Greece and Rome the female body lacked appeal. To them, women were only meant to bare children, not love, cherish, adore, respect, or have interesting, stimulating conversations with.

This apathy towards European women transcended their earlier civilizations. All across Europe women were raped, tortured, maimed and killed by their men. Many European men took great pleasure in watching their women burn at the stake. To get rid of a nagging wife all one needed to do is accuse her of being a witch and Christian ministers, bishops and other men, would gladly torture and kill her. 'The inquisition' lasted from around the mid 1500 to the Salem witch trials in America. Over these centuries Millions of European women were sadistically raped, tortured and killed. It was Fathers who taught their sons to devalue and control their sisters, mothers and all women. Around the late 18th century the widespread, torturous murders of European women stopped, but their overt subjugation continued.

Feminism came forth from the European woman's basic human rights; a want to simply exist. Sound familiar? It literally took centuries for European males to even consider quoting the wedding vows we hear them spewing out today. The term barefoot, pregnant and in the kitchen has still been a real part of European women's lives. They had no place outside of the home. Now, they are determined not to go back to this 'Dark Age'. And like anything that's been withheld for so long, when it's finally obtained people have a tendency to gorge themselves on it. They fear never getting it again. Could you blame European women for going overboard with feminism? Could you blame them if they really did hate men? Regardless, they now feel that it's their turn to dominate White males. Although unable to physically burn men at the stake, they now burn them financially and emotionally. They've developed a lust for power.

Betty Friedman is credited with starting the feminist movement as a response to the overt sexism and sexual harassment that ran rapid in European culture. History overwhelmingly concludes that European men who have the economic power over women will use that power to leverage sex from their female employees, subordinates and any other woman in their zone, every chance they get. Of course this behavior dates back to old Europe, and as European males spread out across the globe, they took their sexual imperative with them.

Most women, who are the head of millions of households, will work any job, no matter how strenuous or degrading, to provide food and shelter for their children. But Receiving rent money isn't enough for a lot of landlords. Time and time again women are forced to open their doors and share their beds with the property owner or face eviction from his land.

During slavery, White men were so used to sneaking out of their beds and running down to the slave quarters to rape their enslaved women that the practice continued long after their physical enslavement was said to be over. White property owners believed they controlled whoever and whatever was on their property.

Douglas A. Blackmon talks about an event that took place among white property owner's years after slavery:

A White mob seized an African Methodist Episcopal minister in Leesburg, Georgia named Rev. W.W. Williams that spring after he began to emerge among local Blacks in the farming community as an influential leader. White men owned all the areas land and were accustomed to the same conjugal rights with Black women on their farms as had existed during antebellum slavery. Rev. Williams began preaching that Black women should resist the sexual advances of the dominant White men in the community, wrote Rev. J.E. Sistruck, in an account of the attack sent to the Department of Justice. "The mob….went upon him without warning and taken him out of the parsonage and stripped him naked and one sat upon his head and each by turns with a buggy whip, whipped him until his back was raw from head to foot and after whipping him they told him that they whipped him because he was controlling colored women." *(Douglass A. Blackmon p.243)*

Just as in slavery, sexual harassment gave the most deprived, White males power. Do you believe Senator Strom Thurmond's young, teenage, Black servant, living in the segregated South, working for a prominent White family, willingly laid down for him? Hell no. The rapes of Black women were so rampant one Governor of South Carolina (Cole Blease) asserted it was the nature of every Black woman to want sex at every opportunity. "Adultery seems to be their favorite pastime." He said "I have …very serious doubts as to weather the crime of rape can be committed against a Negro." Slavery by Another Name, p 305

It was clearly a racist statement intended to cover up criminal assaults against Black women by White males. I found it amusing that such a statement comes from a fool whose female ancestors were forced to wear chastity belts because they couldn't keep their legs closed, and whose ancestors invented prostitution and pedophilia in the first place. It further exposes the code of silence and compliance Southern White males lived by. The feminist movement, women's suffrage and others, was the only alternative defense against these predatory

White males.

I once worked on a military base for a company in Norfolk called Macsons. Macsons supervisors and superintendents had sexual harassment down to a science. This gang of older, White men who were in positions of authority filled their job sites with Black and White single mothers who desperately needed employment. On demolition jobs the supervisors would hand pick women from temporary agencies that they thought would be easiest to manipulate into sexual relationships; a well known European practice.

The most aggressive and foul mouthed of these predator supervisors was a fifty-something year old, married man by the name of Bill Saunders. Bill was a 5'4" loud mouth, repulsive looking man who's every word reeked of illiteracy. But everything Bill Saunders lacked in knowledge and statue he more than made up for in ego. Under no circumstances would he ever admit to being wrong and would terminate anyone with a descending opinion. My first day on the job, Bill introduced me to a young, Black woman named Kim whom he constantly referred to as his assistant and protégée. I was told to report to her if I had any questions or problems on the job. Kim was a single mother of four from one of the local housing projects. She had been a temporary employee until Bill plucked her from a group of temps and hired her as his underling. As the days went by it became abundantly clear that Kim was more then just Bill's assistant; she was his puppet, his gopher, his flunky and his sex partner.

Bill would occasionally, and in public view, message Kim's shoulders and cuddle up next to her on lunch breaks. But as in the nature of any predator, Kim's shoulders weren't the only ones he rubbed. There were over a dozen women on that construction site and Bill Saunders made sure he touched or groped them all. His vulgar, inappropriate comments were an everyday occurrence.

This work environment became unbearable for one particular employee who had the guts to report this predator. As a result Bill Saunders was escorted off the premises by military police and told not to return. I'm sure his absence was a relief for over a dozen women who only wanted to work and go home. After Bill's abrupt departure, Kim became just another employee and eventually an Ex-employee. After all those months her compliance yielded little reward.

However, I do wonder if Kim regrets opening her legs up to such a grungy, manipulative, little man? Or does any woman regret bending over for a short term payoff from a boss that attaches sex as a job qualification? Honestly, in some way or another, women have been offered 'dick' ten times a day since they were about thirteen. For the most part when a mans being nice, buying lunch, giving gifts, offering rides or loaning money, he's hoping for a big payoff; sex. Thank God most women say 'no' because if they didn't we could say goodbye to what's left of the family unit.

Bill Saunder's 'privileged boss syndrome' is by no means an isolated incident. Blue collar sexual harassment is rarely discussed, investigated or prosecuted. It is because of predators like him that working class women feel squeezed, cornered and powerless against their boss' exploitation.

All men need be advised: If your wife, girlfriend, mother, sister, daughter, Black or White is in the American workforce, odds are she has been sexually harassed! Weather she's given in to her boss' or supervisor's advances is another story. Weather this horrible economy made her throw her legs up and proclaim "I was just doing what I had to do," is between you and her. But bare in mind that in European culture promotions and raises can come at a very high price and will stretch your integrity to its limits. The sad part is that as much as it goes on today, despite laws and lawsuits, it was ten times worse forty and fifty years ago.

How did something so right go so wrong? Unfortunately, as feminism grew so did its propaganda. A secret agenda circulated among its hierarchy; homosexuality. By the time it became evident, homosexual women were using their feminist platform to promote 'alternate lifestyles' and a so called 'sexual revolution,' the concept had a foothold upon the world.

Homosexuals turned feminism into a divisive tool to serve their same sex agenda. Today, the feminist movement seeks to put a wedge between men and women. Feminists seek power, authority, influence and the last word. They do not believe in 'give and take' with men, but instead complete domination over them. As one doctor put it "Feminists try to make women feel guilty for wanting men," and push homosexuality as their only hope.

Feminism encourages, even demands promiscuity. To empower women

24

feminism expects them to think and behave like men. I even see talk shows and radio programs promoting swinging parties; telling women to have multiple boyfriends and multiple sex partners. Europeans use and equate sex with power. No longer is sex a loving, spiritual bonding, but a calculated means to an end. Sigmund Fraud, whom most American psychologists aspire to be, concluded that; "Europeans were motivated by power and sex."

Feminists always compare women to men. The problem is, women weren't meant to be whores, hoes, or sluts; theoretically the male anatomy can handle the abuse. I'm not suggesting that its right, but physically the differences are clear. The abuse to the female body and mind can be tremendous. When it comes to multiple sex partners, a woman's chances of getting a sexually transmitted disease far outweigh that of a man. Festering diseases always affect a woman's reproductive organs first. A woman can't breast feed her child if she has a polluted womb. Men don't even have that type of reproductive tract. Now, take a hard look at the number of women forced to have hysterectomies because of festering diseases, infection, tubel pregnancies, and terminated pregnancies, then tell me that it's alright for women to have multiple sex partners. Sadly, abortion clinics are filled with the victims of this feminist propaganda. There's no chance of a man getting pregnant accidentally and being forced to make such a heart wrenching decision.

Trust me, being with a woman who's been with five men compared to one who's been with forty-five, feels totally different sexually. Think about it realistically; can an average Joe sexually satisfy a female porn star who's been with over 600 men and a horse? No matter what a man says, he doesn't want to marry a woman who's seen more penises' then a doctor at the Norfolk Health Department. A husband can derive little pleasure from a wife with a battered and beaten womb. And a loose woman has no devotion to a family structure. Disloyalty outside the home inspires disloyalty inside the home. The so called sexual revolution never told women about the psychological affects of promiscuous behavior. Married couples who share what's called an open marriage or swinger's lifestyle aren't really married. They're husband and wife on paper only; much like a business arrangement. A swinging couple says "our bodies weren't meant for each other exclusively."

"The earlier a woman begins to have sex, she increases the number of sex partners she'll have over her lifespan. She also increases the likelihood of diseases, low wage jobs, and confusing

sex with friendship."
-Henry Makow,PHD.

She'll come to believe friendship requires sex.
And in case you've never noticed, feminist never, ever mention the word LOVE!

Hate filled feminists

Although some feminists were abused by their fathers or other men they loved, most of them are the products of their fathers being abused by their mothers. Confused? Take note; most feminists revere their mothers and hate their fathers. Why? Because the mother always berated and belittled the father in front of them. A girl child watching her mother humiliate and blame her father for her own failures, frustrations and lack of achievement, will begin to side with her mother and begins to dislike or disrespect her own father and other men.

 The father appears weak. As I said before, children usually admire and/or emulate the dominant parent. Violent parents leave scars on their children's minds. Remember, all arguments are mentally videotaped and often replayed by your children. Never fight and argue in front of your children because they are subconsciously choosing sides and forming lifelong opinions. Most of these girls grow up in constant debate or obstinacy with men.

Sometimes disguised with spunky catchphrases like 'girl power' the anti-men movement is constantly in your face. And now, feminisms main objective is to take women out of the home, period.

"Those who want to destroy the family will continue to urge mothers to leave the home and become 'fulfilled in the workplace.' When the mother goes into the workplace to become 'fulfilled', or to increase the family's income, she leaves the care of the children to others. Those who warn against such practices will continue to be scorned by the feminists and others who have a hidden agenda: they want to destroy the family." –The New World Order, pp245-246 by Ralph Epperson 1990'

As we've witnessed for too many years in Black culture, where the man has been methodically plucked or driven from the home, the Black mother assumes responsibilities that God and nature bestowed upon the man. The male archetype is no longer a force within the household and the impressionable boy/girl pieces together a father figure or male role model based upon television, music videos and males they see on the street or who happen to cross their paths. It's why young men don't know how to treat women and young girls have no idea how they're supposed to be treated by their boyfriends or husbands. Its irrefutable evidence that not just the Black family but society as a whole suffers from a fragmented household.

As I've previously given irrefutable evidence that conspiracies do exist and effect all of our lives, one can only surmise that to ignore such outright attacks on the family unit by homosexual-zealot-feminists is absolutely insane. Although feminism is only one weapon homosexuals use to subdue women, its effectiveness on White women has proven catastrophic. Because of their Matriarchal ancestry, Black women historically weren't subjugated by their men anywhere near the historical accounts of their White counterparts. It's what made the European woman's rebellion more intense. But European cultural effects cannot be ignored. Feminism's tentacles are far reaching and have infected the psyche of women of all races, the world over. This threat is very real.

Henry Makow made a stoic assessment. *"People without stable families are easy to distract and control… "(The Illuminati") 'extolled' sexual liberation because promiscuous women are less dedicated to family, and less attractive and suitable as wives and mothers. Furthermore if sex is freely available, men have less incentive to marry or be faithful…In America, the cultural measure of a woman's value is her sex appeal. (As this asset depreciates quickly, she is neurotically obsessed with appearance and plagued by weight problems.) …As an adolescent, her role model is Britney Spears, a singer whose act approximates a strip tease. From Britney, she learns that she will be loved only if she gives sex. Thus, she learns to "hook up" rather than to demand patient courtship and true love. As a result, dozens of males know her before her husband does. She loses her innocence, which is part of her charm. She becomes hardened and calculating. Unable to love, she is unfit to receive her husband's seed."*

The casual use of the word 'sexy' has always annoyed me. When you refer to someone as being 'sexy' you're essentially saying that you and/or others view them as someone you only want to have sex with. You immediately objectify that person as a 'thing' for yours and others sexual gratification. Forget about substance, brains or personality, they're here to serve the purpose of someone's orgasm. The word 'sexy' is one dimensional and telling someone that they're 'sexy' really isn't a compliment at all. When a woman/man accepts being called 'sexy' they're satisfied with the knowledge someone out there wants to have sex with them. Simply uttering the words "you are beautiful" is by far an absolute compliment!

It is important to remember; <u>there is no superiority between the sexes. They are opposites who are equal. Nature formed this balance in order to create life and sustain life. The balance between masculine and feminine energies must be acknowledged, accepted, respected and strived for in every aspect of our lives. One sex trying to suppress, overpower, manipulate, outdo and 'battle' the other puts nature out of harmony and keeps the world unbalanced and created the mixed up society we live in today. This world urgently needs families. It needs men and women who love, respect and compliment each other.</u>

Destroy the family and society as we know it will crumble. The next time you hear a feminist say "women don't need sex they're just doing men a favor," you're reply should be "no, they're actually doing homosexuals a favor."

B.) Experimentation

<u>Experiment;</u> 1.A test made to demonstrate a known truth, examine the validity of a hypothesis, or determine the nature of something. 2. To try something new

<u>Stupid;</u> 1.Slow to learn or understand. 2. Lacking intelligence. 3. in a stunned or dazed state. 4. Pointless; worthless.

Sex and drugs are the two biggest social experiments of which people love to boast. It is indicative of the dysfunctional society in which we live. When you're young, we all have impressionable minds that convince our bodies that we're invincible, 'nothing bad is going to happen' and 'you're only young once'. You rarely hear about older people experimenting with sex or drugs because once maturity kicks in their interests change. Young people want to be involved in everything and not be left out of anything; especially if it sounds fun or exciting. The hierarchy of American culture knows this and has divided its citizens into demographic categories which make them easy to distract, control, and indoctrinate.

It's hard to stand alone and since few are willing to 'buck' the system, like sheep they willingly file into groups that will accept them. Once accepted into a 'click' the rationalization for stupid behavior begins. Pop culture has become the gold standard that breeds experimentation. "Everybody's doing it!" is the enduring, subliminal catch phrase of this century.

Television, also called "tell-lie-vision" by some, is the number one source of propaganda consistently promoting homosexual ideas. They push the homosexual agenda onto impressionable, young girls like a pharmaceutical company pushing pills. It is methodical. It is consistent. It is relentlessly in your face 24 hours a day. Songs like "I kissed a girl" gets heavy rotation and demands the public be more open minded.

Television, also called "the idiot box" by some, is controlled by a handful of people who are able to force their reality upon countless millions around the world. Young minds are the most susceptible to cultural trends, subliminal messages, propaganda and outright distortion. Talent, or should I say the lack there of, is replaced by instant celebrity as soon as one stands in front of a camera and professes homosexuality to the world. Homosexuals have changed their tactics to adapt to globalization and the 'new world order.'

Lesbian and feminist campaigns new strategy focus' less on "girl power" inside the home to; "single women without men, have more fun outside the home." This new, less aggressive tactic takes the emphasis off confrontation with men to joviality with women. More times than not, experimentation can lead to internalization. This seemingly 'innocent' experimentation among young women, no matter how trivial it seems to them, awakens and arouses their most basic sexual desires; it stimulates the libido. Even on the most rudimentary level, a pleasant lesbian experience, even something seemingly as harmless as a kiss, will make an impressionable, young woman excited enough to share that experience more enthusiastically with others. This offers an amusing yet underlying acceptance of the behavior and invites more explicit experimentation; thus condoning the act itself.

c.) A.I.D.S.

There is no doubt the paralyzing images associated with A.I.D.S. had a lasting psychological effect on women. It was the type of fear that transcended color, religion or class. And as rumors and misinformation grew; news reports pointed to heterosexual sex as the number one culprit as it spread among the female population. In the mid 80's women began to religiously force their sex partners to use condoms or simply closed their legs altogether; opting for celibacy. I spoke to dozens of women who despite how much they loved men hadn't had sex in years. Fear seems to last a lot longer then love. And by now I'm guessing every woman in America over age 25 knows someone who died of this disease; including other women. Lesbians seized the opportunity to fill the emotional void left in the lives of these vulnerable mothers and daughters who were in need of companionship, financial assistance, excitement and even pleasure.

By the mid 1990's and just as women we're overcoming these fears and re-evaluating the natural order of male/female relationships, Black women saw a new, more sinister threat rear its ugly head; the 'homo-thug'.

Homo-thug: Is a homosexual male who dates or enters into relationships with women while secretly having sex with males. **Homo-thugs** don't consider themselves homosexual because some of them (not all) don't allow themselves to be penetrated but will ram their penises into any orifice another male has to offer. **Homo-thugs** are often immersed in the hip-hop world. They usually dress in the latest street wear, use street vernacular and portray a hard-core masculine image which enables them to blend naturally into urban culture.

The following is a chain of events that will make you shutter- a related interesting and compelling chapter of events relating to A.I.D.S and its looming fear among women in the Black community. I was compelled to share this information with you. The following pages are excerpts from his book:

"In 1999 I stumbled into the restroom of a local night club to take a leak. I was heavily intoxicated and thereafter intended to go home and sleep it off. About three minutes later two young Black guys walked in. They were arguing and I glanced over my shoulder to make sure they weren't anywhere near me in case a fight ensued. That's when I heard one of them say "shhhhh" and gestured that I could be listening to their conversation. Then one of them turned to me and boldly asked:

"Yo man, you don't give a fuck what we're talkin' 'bout; do ya?"
"Hell naw!," I replied to his odd question.
As I zipped up my pants and walked over to the sink, I heard that same voice say with authority;
"I don't care what your wife says; you're coming home with me tonight. Tell her I'm too drunk to drive or something," he demanded.

In surprise, I turned around to see these two young males embraced in a kiss that would have made Little Richard blush. I was shocked. I dried my hands on my pants as I backed out of the bathroom. I didn't want either of them looking at my ass. These two twenty-something year old males were in the bathroom making out while one of their unsuspecting wives was sitting at a table in the next room. Until that night I was oblivious to the fact that brothers with corn rolls, sagging jeans, and Timberland boots could be gay. I shook my head and got the hell out of there. That's his wife's problem to deal with, I thought.

In 2004, I ran into an old friend of mine named Kenny. Kenny and I use to work together at one of the worst factories in Tidewater. It was a horrible place to be employed during the summer months; hot, sticky, dusty and toxic. The racially divisive atmosphere developed and nurtured by our employer, actually brought many of us closer; as with myself and Kenny. Usually the highpoint of Kenny's day was his young, beautiful, teenage daughter Trisha bringing him lunch. They only lived a few blocks away and his only child Trisha would fix him hot plates and deliver them at twelve o'clock sharp.

Sometimes Trisha would stick around and sit with her daddy in the break room as he gobbled it all down.
"Trisha's going to be a heart breaker, man. If I was just two years younger..." I'd tease him.
"Don't make me hurt you. That's my baby girl," he'd smile with a look of pride and joy

that only a father could give or understand. It's the kind of face all fathers have when they talk about their little girls. Trisha loved to draw and sketch. Kenny told me her dream was to go to college, study fashion and become a shoe and clothes designer; someday start her own business. Kenny bragged about her 3.8 grade point average, so I knew college was very much possible.

Seeing my old friend after so many years, at a car wash of all places, was a surprise. I felt bad we hadn't kept in touch. Immediately after we shook hands, the first thing I wanted to know was how's little Trisha? I'd heard through the grapevine she'd breezed through college and was working her dream job at a known footwear manufacturing company. I heard she even had a company car. Kenny stared down at the ground for a few seconds then coldly replied;
"Dead."
"What the hell are you talking about?" I gasped.
"Trisha died from A.I.D.S. almost a year ago."

Kenny went on to explain to me how his daughter fell in love with a boy she'd met in college. As it turns out this boy was bi-sexual (a term coined by gay males to ease the shame of being called homosexual) and didn't tell Trisha he was cheating on her with other males. Kenny also told me he suspected the boy knew he was infected but didn't tell his daughter a dam thing. So my next question was;
"What happened to the boy?"
"He lives in Hampton," Kenny mumbled.
"Lives!" I exclaimed.
"For now," Kenny nodded with the same cold look in his eyes.
Once again, my old friend shook my hand and quickly drove away.
He was broken. And he knew that no matter what he did it wouldn't bring his little girl back. I couldn't imagine losing something so precious the way in which he lost her. But I'll always remember Trisha as the beautiful, young woman who use to bring her daddy those hot lunches. I also think about the two young homosexual males from the club that night. It could easily have been one of them who infected Trisha with A.I.D.S. Kenny's little girl had been done in by the 'homo-thug.'

Homo-thugs help make A.I.D.S. the number one killer of Black women (ages 19-35) in America today. Seventy-six percent of all women infected with A.I.D.S are through heterosexual sex. On a scale of tragic, urban disasters to strike the Black community I'd label this one a category 5. Young women from college campuses to church pulpits aren't safe from these predators. This egregious Black on Black crime should be in the forefront of every conversation, every debate, every news story, and every church sermon. Yeah, I called it a Black on Black crime because that's exactly what it is. An infected Black man knowingly deceiving a Black woman about his sexual orientation and his HIV status is criminal.

Is it mere loneliness or desperation that will cause a woman to stay with a man whom she suspects is "on the down low?" A lonely, desperate woman needs self-esteem and counseling, not a homosexual male. An old friend of mine named Tina told me her suspicions concerning her boyfriend Roodie. It seemed Roodie had been incarcerated for a few years and upon his release Tina decided they would reconcile, resume their relationship and move in together. Roodie was released from prison after five years on a drug charge. He assured Tina he'd never sell drugs again. A month or so after his release of course, he was back on the street selling drugs. But that wasn't the problem.

Tina told me Roodie's behavior had drastically changed since his incarceration. Five years earlier he was quiet, cool, and fun to be around. Now it seemed he was a loud, brash, gun-toting thug. Tina said she didn't mind the thug in him, but it was the feminine traits he exhibited at rather odd times that were disturbing. One night she and a friend were on their way to the store but Tina forgot her check card. When she arrived back home unexpectedly, she found Roodie nestled nervously on the couch while a buddy of his sat stiffly next to him. She said the peculiar thing was that, and I quote, "the whole room smelled like shit."

   Tina and I had been friends since I was nineteen years old. And we shared a lot of experiences with each other over the years. So when she asked my opinion of her boy friends peculiar behavior I told her to dump him and move on. But as usual Tina never listened to me. We all know people who'll ask you for advice but never take it. Two weeks later she called me again to get my opinion on yet another peculiar incident. This time she made me swear I wouldn't breathe a word of it to anyone, and I haven't until now. (I'm a writer with an ax to grind; besides I changed their names).

It seems the previous night as she and Roodie were lying next to each other in bed, Roodie began to make strange, erotic moaning sounds in his sleep. Suddenly, this hard core, ex- con, drug dealer had a bowel movement right there in the middle of the bed. After I finished laughing (just like I'm doing now) I told Tina I'd never heard of anything like that in my life. I also told her she had balls for telling anybody about that incident. And what was my opinion and subsequent advice? I told her that her boyfriend was having a gay wet dream and relaxed his ass muscles, if it's called that, and couldn't avoid the after effects. I instructed Tina to put that 'stranger' out of her life immediately and go get tested. I say stranger because he was clearly not the same guy she fell in love with before he entered the prison system.

Would you believe she stayed with him another two months before she left? She wasn't just hard headed, she was stupid! Tina was playing Russian roulette with her life. The cloaked homo-thug depends desperately on a woman's need for him. He revels in the fact that she won't snoop or ask tough questions. The more he can explain his way out of questionable behavior, the bolder his deceptive, deadly conduct becomes. Like any predator that smells weakness or vulnerability, he preys on her emotions.

These predators can be anyone and everywhere at anytime, because like the chameleon, they blend in. But how are homo-thugs able to manipulate so many Black women into having unprotected sex? Truth is, a lot of smart and observant Black women are purposely closing their eyes to the facts. The sooner Black women accept the fact that Black men on the "down-low" and homo-thugs are both predators then they are equipped to deal with them as such. Predators prey on the weak and count heavily on a person not knowing they're around.

Black women have to look for answers outside the perimeter of their relationships if they intend to survive this crisis. They must ask the tough questions and demand straight answers. Starting with the question; "Is his dick worth dying for?" As soon as he unzips his pants that's the first question that should pop into a woman's head. Then she must follow up, snoop and be nosy. Do whatever it takes. She must understand that it's her life at stake. Women must face the fact that the homo-thug hates her as much as their sexually confused minds hate themselves. Why else would he withhold life or death knowledge from the woman he professes love for? Ladies and gentlemen I give you another wrinkle on the fat belly of self hate.

Over the next ten years an estimated 600,000 black men will be released from prison. The problem is that some of them are no longer men. If you're a Black man in prison do you really think that because you're in a cage you must behave like an animal? You don't. If I told you that with one collect call you could save your sister's life, right there from your prison cell, would you do it? Would you make that one telephone call? Well, your sister is in grave danger from your cellmate. That's right; the guy in the cell next to you gave up his manhood when he went to prison. Every night other inmates pass his him around like a cigarette.

Yet every Saturday his wife and kids come to visit him. He kisses his wife's lips probably with the stink of another man's testicles still on his breath. His wife has no idea he gave up his manhood a long time ago. But you do. You know he's no longer anal-retentive, and it turns your stomach to see him in that visiting area hugged up with that loyal, devoted woman, pretending like he's done nothing wrong. As soon as he's released, he's going straight back to that woman and infect her with A.I.D.S. That's right; he's planning to kill her! Doesn't she have a right to decide whether she wants to die or not?
He's certainly not going to tell her he was having sex with men in prison.

Fact: The 600,000 newly released inmates are going straight back to your old neighborhoods to visit your sisters, daughters, and mothers. You may call home one night and find out your former cellmate is sitting right next to your ex- wife or child's mother. Then what are you going to do?

You must pick up the phone and call all the women your homosexual cellmate deals with. You don't have to tell them who you are, just tell them that their lives are in danger and why. You can send them an e-mail or get their addresses and send an anonymous letter. Within the community itself the activities of the homo-thug m8ust be reported to the Black woman who will ultimately be affected and infected by his callous disregard for her life.

Most importantly, before any woman pulls back the sheets to have welcome home sex with her ex-con boyfriend or husband, she must first make him submit to an A.I.D.S. test. Take him to your personal care physician or at the very least, the public health department, let the doctor swab his mouth, and wait for the results. If he loves you and has nothing to hide he won't complain. But if he fights you tooth and nail then he could be trying to kill you; run!

All women who are concerned about their health, safety and well being must study **'The Tells'**. A lot of women overlook the obvious to ease the pain of having no one in their lives. In dealing with the homo-thug some give-a- ways are common sense; other **'Tells'** are harder to read. Here are a few obvious signs **(Tells)** that something is wrong.

If you visit your man in jail and his hair is freshly greased and braided, there's a problem. Obviously there are no women in there with him. Therefore a man must have braided his hair. No real man would allow another man to grease his scalp let alone braid his hair.

Does he seem nonchalant about going to jail and says "baby don't bond me out, I'll just stay in here until my court date." Stay in there and do what exactly?

Does he go to the message parlor and prefer a man rubbing his back instead of a woman? If a man lets another man rub his back at a message parlor, he'll let a man rub his back at home in his bedroom.

Does he prefer spending quality time with his guy friends more so than with his woman?

At the rate this disease is destroying the Black community these are just a handful of the questions Black women should be asking about the men in their lives. Believe me; it breaks God's heart every time a man she created thinks he's a woman. I imagine it's much like the feeling a mother gets the day she finds out the man-child she gave birth to is no longer a man. If it is in fact true that 70% of Black women are unwed, the Black community has a very serious problem."

D.) Displacement

I see females impersonating men and behaving like male chauvinists; some are even walking around with their pants sagging off their behinds. Men carrying babies on their backs and worrying about manicures, while women scream 'I don't need a man' and molds her boy child into her image. Our entire Society has become functionally **displaced**. Life goes on but the men and women who interact in this society are completely dislocated from normalcy, from nature and from their ancestral roles. The primary and essential function of the woman as **nurturer - protector** has overlapped with the man's designation of **hunter-gatherer**. The overprotective single mother doesn't allow her 'boy' to hunt from fear he might skin his knee and the male hunters are now metro-sexual, afraid to pick up a spear because they might break a nail. Women throughout this society are disproportionately **displaced**; detached from the natural order of things. Yet their displacement mirrors, or some say was a response to this country's male catastrophe.

We'll address the rudimentary cause of aggressive, female behaviors later. However, in closing this chapter, a crisis in the mother –son relationship must be discussed to some degree. When a father abandons the home and his responsibilities, it leaves the woman in a precarious position. A woman who is forced to assume the father's role in the home must acknowledge the far reaching effects spoiling has on her child. And by spoil I mean to mess up, ruin and destroy.

How do you ruin a child? You pamper, pander or indulge far too many of their wants and you enact little if any disciplinary measures other then raising your voice. The child's moral fiber will eventually decay as they become masters at scheming and controlling a weak parent. This means catastrophe for a male child as well as devastation for society. He's already become lazy and devalues women as pawns in his means to an end. He essentially becomes a taker with nothing to offer the world. He never learns to provide for anyone other then himself, and when he attempts to take care of himself it's by means of usury. You can never do enough for a spoiled child because he/she will always want more and more and more.

Once your spoiled, manipulative boy reaches adulthood, he leaves home and finds a woman who will cater and take care of him like his mother. In most cases he will drain her emotionally and financially dry, before moving back home. A spoiled boy becomes a man whose mother seems to be omnipresent throughout his relationships. Many spoiled boys never get their lives together. Incapable of making it on their own, they entertain schemes and pipe dreams that lead nowhere. Sadly, far too many end up in jail or easily inducted into religion or philosophies that cater to their subjugation and usury of women; all because of the lasting, crippling effect of a mother's spoilage- displacing her own son.

When a male child doesn't know or wasn't taught his role in society as a man, he can be easily indoctrinated or made to believe that the female role is also his role; enter homosexuality. However, let's be clear, the displacement of men in society has been equally matched by the displacement of women.

E.) Betrayal

A woman catches her man cheating and feels so angry that she decides a female relationship is her only alternative. Honestly, there isn't much that can be said about a woman who runs into the arms of a female because a man betrayed her trust. It is a ridiculous rationale that a female lover won't cheat or be disrespectful. Usually there are pre- existing emotional or psychological problems that send people to these extremes. A woman who gets continuously 'dogged out' by men in every relationship blames all of mankind instead of her knack for attracting and entering into relationships with the wrong type of men. A woman who thinks a female lover can't cheat or be abusive suffers from a chronic case of stupidity.

Where Do Butch-Dykes Come From?

Butch/dyke/ bull-dagger: Refers to a female who acts and dresses like a man but who vigorously pursues relationships with very feminine females. Although considered disrespectful terms, many homosexual females are frequently referenced as such.

Lesbian: Derived from the Greek occupied island of Lesbos; an island for women only, it is a term exclusive to homosexual females.

This form of displacement in women is truly heartbreaking. Was there too much testosterone, pheromones, estrogen or X chromosomes that causes this actual physical and mental condition? That's inconclusive. However, there's a difference between homosexuality in women being on the rise and what we're currently experiencing; a spike. A spike suggests it's been caused by a specific, precise source.

Where do butch-dykes come from? That's the most common question people ask about this type of homosexual female. Once again, the origin of women dressing and behaving like men has its roots in ancient Greece. In homosexual Greek culture, women often dressed like men in order to get their husbands to have sex with them. A vast majority of Greek males were so drawn to young boys and other males that they exhibited a total lack of attraction to their own wives. Centuries later the reason has changed but the technique remains the same.

Today, in a male dominated society butch-dykes feel that they are commanding respect within their community by dressing and acting like men. But their main objective is to project a strong sense of security and masculinity to women. Since females are naturally attracted to males, as nature designed, butch-dykes intend to get an edge on men when it comes to the courtship of woman. They imitate all the natural male characteristics in hopes that women will perceive them as men. They believe this male persona will assure women that they are just as capable and possess all the qualities of a real man. In their mind behaving like a man enables them to ward off danger as well as competition from male suitors who may be interested in their "woman."

 In most situations that involve any form of physicality, from blue collar work to sexual relations, butch-dykes go out of their way to establish dominance over men. When people are around, the butch-dyke exhibits what can be referred to as an 'alter- ego'. She takes herself out of being female and puts on a male mask. With the internal fears of a man taking her woman and not being able to physically compete with men, the butch-dyke overcompensates by being loud, obnoxious and keeps the focus of most conversations on her sexual prowess in comparison to men. Any man who has ever engaged in a dispute with the so called "butch-dyke' usually finds himself in a precarious position. He can't fight her because underneath the manly facade there's a female, and most men are taught not to hit a woman. But if he does decide to engage in a physical altercation, he'll be branded as a man who beats up on girls. If that's not bad enough, if she ends up kicking his butt, people will say "he got his ass whipped by a woman." Try living that down. A lot of men feel that if "she thinks she's a man I'm gone treat her like a man!" But because of homosexual legislation, no matter who was the aggressor, he could still be charged with a hate crime. It allows butch-dykes to be as aggressive as they like without any consequences. Add in the pity factor they garner from living in a confused state of mind and it becomes a lose-lose situation for most men.

Yet another and more obvious reason for the physical characteristics of the butch/dyke is society's one sided, Eurocentric description of beauty. Quite a few butch/dykes actually do look like men. And they've been told they were ugly for so long they stopped trying to look feminine and whole heartedly embraced their masculine traits. The beauty of their mothers and grandmothers were dismantled and replaced by a lie and illusion. They've internalized self hate. Dressing like a man is not the cure for self hate. I use to laugh whenever I saw a woman dressed like a man, spitting, cursing, holding herself and trying to act hard. Now, I no longer laugh, I feel pity. There's no sight more heart wrenching then seeing a young woman dressed like a man, and having her pants 'sagging' off her behind.

Resigned by her lack of sex appeal, a butch-dyke will parade her female partner around in public to validate her alternative lifestyle. This ploy draws attention away from her European perceived ugliness and onto her 'sexy' female partner. She not only wants men to envy her catch but 'respect her game'. When attention is paid to her partner, by extension, the respect she was previously denied is given to her. Even straight women will wonder how she was able to lure such an attractive female. She'll now internally feel validated for her sex-style, and contend that she is winning her competition against men for the affection and attention of the more gentile sex.

Note: It is important to remember, butch-dykes aren't trying to be men, they're trying to replace men.

**Why do women who don't want men, go out and
get women who look like men?**

In a word; confused. Once again I must reiterate the fact that we all live in a society that
has been displaced. Homosexuality itself is the mutation of displacement. But you must
realize that the human mind has a strong drive to correct itself. Since it is an unnatural
state of existence for two females to be romantically involved with each other, it's easier
to dress one up and pretend she's a man. The natural pheromones, muscles, facial hair,
clothes, walk and mannerisms nature designed to make opposites attract are now
disguised by improvised acting, crew cuts, clothes and cologne. These 'props' help to
make the more feminine homosexual female attracted to the masculine homosexual
female. Within herself she has created the illusion of a protective male companion. To
qualify this unnatural imbalance within her own psyche a woman chooses the butch-
dyke to compensate for the loss of masculine energy; thus making it a little bit easier to
turn her back on actual males.

When it comes to homosexuality, for the most part females differ from males. Lesbians
are more emotionally charged while their male counterparts are extremely testosterone
driven. Homosexual males want to 'stick' something or be 'poked' and prodded because
males are built to climax physically. Woman climax mentally. Women in general aren't
anywhere near as interested in penetration as men think.

It's amusing to listen to immature men talk about lesbians. When a man hears that a
woman's 'gay' the first thing he says is "oh, she just ain't been with the right man. She
ain't had none of this dick." He speaks as if his sexual prowess is the solution to female
homosexuality. Nothing could be further from the truth. Since climaxing is
psychological for woman anyway, the butch-dykes, being females themselves, are doing
everything men are not. These manly females are giving the emotional support woman
need and climaxing is included because it was psychological to begin with. Mental
penetration and climaxing is seldom achieved or discussed by today's testosterone
driven male population.

Butch-dykes shoulder the responsibilities men run away from. Men stopped taking care
of the home and women got tired of taking anything the men did to them. Yesterday's
woman was raised thinking that her feelings didn't matter. She didn't have her needs
satisfied. She physically and mentally "faked it." Who knows better what a woman
wants more than another woman? Butch-dykes use this to their advantage. After sex, the

butch-dyke isn't going to turn over and go to sleep. She's going to try and make the overall experience something a man can't measure up to. She's going to cuddle, kiss her forehead and put the female ahead of herself. They are going to bond emotionally. Their interactions go beyond mere pillow talk. Unfortunately, men still don't listen. Women find it easier to talk about their feelings with other women.

A Woman is built to respond to a real man and when she doesn't have a real man to take the lead she looks elsewhere. But men must never forget; a 'man' is also built to submit to his woman. While he exhibits his manhood to the rest of the world, the strength of his relationship lies within the reciprocity of submission. Men who feel as if nothing else is required because their paying the bills, will continue to lose their women to the butch-dyke. The butch-dyke is giving your woman her undivided attention while you do all your thinking with your penis. She's listening, caring, caressing and reassuring. A man must learn to sex his woman's mind as well as her body. Sometimes a woman really does just want to be held.

Homosexuality & Survival Sex

Survival Sex: Having sex as a means to get through a crisis and/or a perceived dangerous situation or circumstance beyond one's control of threats, real or imagined.

The constantly changing street culture has coined a term called '**survival sex**.' Some males who have sex with other males for money or fear and not enjoyment do not consider themselves homosexual. They think that because the emotional attachment is missing, the homosexual stigma evaporates and the homosexual act itself is void; wrong. Whether you are trading sex for money, housing, jewelry, crack cocaine on the street or a carton of cigarettes in the penitentiary, it's still homosexual. A same- sex, sex style remains the constant no matter what the situation or environment that produces it.

The link between drugs and homosexuality is nothing new. The power of drugs and sex is strong and has always been potent. Most drugs are ingested to numb our senses to the things that scare us most. Drugs give us excuses for wayward behavior and an escape from some current drama. When a person sells his/her body, they do so to give others physical pleasure in exchange for getting something they feel they need. Trading your body and your self respect in exchange for drugs has its lasting emotional effect but it also destroys your ethical compass. Prostitution is a major stepping stone into the homosexual realm. When the monkey on your back is hungry, you will feed it by any means.

Committing homosexual acts to support a drug habit makes you homosexual. The rationale behind your commission of the act is inconsequential to the act itself. A lot of women we call 'weed heads' and are addicted to marijuana will smoke a 'blunt' with any one who rolls it up. In exchange, many of them understand that sex or a sexual act comes with the territory. If you go to a job with a lot of female 'weed heads', they've already been with most of their fellow employees. In a number of women, marijuana acts as an aphrodisiac. So not only are they prone to be with men but women as well. Having a husband or boyfriend is secondary and is rationalized when it comes to a female supporting a drug habit. This

43

is another example of survival sex.

My ex-girlfriend's daughter wanted to leave home but she lacked the job skills or intelligence to take care of her self. She was spoiled and made an easy target for the predatory 'butch-dyke' female. Her lack of interpersonal skills, common sense, a steady income, and shelter, made her choose a homosexual relationship in order to survive.

Yet another example of survival sex is Hollywood. A lot of survival sex takes place behind the scenes; both heterosexual and homosexual. Many of your favorite stars are not just claiming to be 'gay' but committing homosexual acts as a way to survive in a tightly controlled atmosphere of perversion. To obtain movie roles producers and directors make sure the 'casting couch' turns both ways. Actors in Hollywood are chosen by higher ups to be stars as long as their bodies are on stand by. It's usually all pre-decided.

Take a good look at all the celebrities who defy the odds and make it. The first thing that happens is the homosexual hierarchy will send a famous homosexual to befriend them, advise them, whisper in their ear and ultimately, seduce them. The music and hip-hop industry works the exact same way. In fact, quite a few of your favorite, hardcore, gangster rappers are homosexuals with casting couches of their own.

Casting couch: An old Entertainment term meaning; in order to obtain certain movie roles or music contracts the perspective actor, actress, singer, etc. must have sex or perform a sex act with the director, producer, music mogul, etc. in exchange for opportunity.

Games Homosexuals Play

Mental disorder: is a psychological or behavioral pattern that occurs in an individual and is thought to cause distress or disability that is not expected as a part of normal development or culture. Wikipedia

Self indulge: The need to satisfy ones one appetite and desires.

The homosexual creed is sex without responsibility. That is why bath houses public restrooms steam rooms and underground sex clubs has always been popular among homosexual males. They may seem uncoof to us but these are places homosexual can engage in anonymous oral and anal sex with complete strangers and when the encounter is over, they can both go about their business. You don't think the village people were singing about the YMCA because they like working out. I went to the YMCA in the Gent section of Norfolk, and was approached by several homosexual males my first day there. They simply didn't care.

I remember when Republican Senator Lary Craig was in an airport restroom rubbing his right foot against the left foot of a guy in the stall next to him. It was one of a few signals pre-arranged by homosexuals to insure that the individual in the stall next to them was there for sex. But instead of getting his hands on his fellow commuter's penis, it was law enforcement conducting a sting. Only the compulsion of a sexual disorder would drive a married, sitting U.S. Senator to risk his career and reputation by walking into such a public place with the intention of putting a total strangers sweaty testacies into his mouth. Unbelievable!

Most homosexuals hate being criticized or taking responsibility for their actions. Weather you are having sex inside your bedroom, behind locked doors or in the back seat of a car parked on a public street, you are still responsible for your actions. Sex entails responsibility. But what if someone was unable to control their sexual impulses? Who then is responsible for their actions; the government?

Their parents? You? Me?

I followed up on research done by the much hated (and a couple of suspect) Dr. Paul Cameron of The **Family Research Institute**. After combining those studies it was calculated that; homosexual males perform oral sex on almost all of their sexual contacts and ingest the seamen from half of them. Seamen contains many of the germs carried in the blood. The homosexual's penis will have often been in unsanitary places such as a rectum. The person involved may become infected with hepatitis A or gonorrhea (and even HIV and hepatitis B.) Most homosexual contact occurs among strangers. Homosexuals average between 106 and 1105 different partners a year. That is a minimum of two sex partners a week or a maximum of 52 per month. Jesus Christ!

Anal sex surveys indicate that about 90% of homosexuals have engaged in anal sex. In a six month long study of daily sexual dairies 3 homosexual men averaged 110 sex partners in 68 rectal encounters a year. With staggering numbers such as these to confront, how do gay rights activist still maintain that most homosexuals are in loving monogamous relationships? Could they be talking about cereal monogamy? That's when someone has a series of relationships one after another.

During anal sex, the rectum becomes a mixing bowl for saliva and its germs and / or an artificial lubricant, the recipients own feces, what ever germs, infection or substance the penis has on it, and the seminal fluid of the inserter. The anal wall is only one cell thick so sperm can easy penetrate and cause immunologic damage. If tearing or bruising occurs, these substances gain almost direct access to the blood stream. During heterosexual sex sperm cannot penetrate the multi layered vagina and no feces is present. Anal sex is probably the most sexually efficient way to spread hepatitis B , HIV, Syphilis and other blood born diseases.

The family research institute also reported that 80% of homosexuals surveyed admitted to licking and/ or inserting their tongue into the anus of partners and thus ingesting medically significant amounts of feces (also known as tossing salads) Those who eat or wallow in it are probably at even greater risk. In the diary study 70% of homosexuals had engaged in this activity. Exposure to fecal discharge of dozens of strangers each year is extremely unhealthy. Note: *A large number of homosexual males are in the food service industry*. Italics mine.

....This greater intensity and perversion is manifest among many of these adult male homosexuals in a practice called "fisting." Fisting is the act of violently ramming one's hand, fist or arm all the way up to the elbow through another's anus opening. Apparently, for both giver and, eventually, receiver, it is sexually stimulating. European progress (or, rather, the rapid return to their original sexual practices) is pervasive in their sexual culture. In their competition to reach the outer limits of sexual exploration, simple sodomy is not enough. To our knowledge, though fisting does not result in death, although there is evidence that the tearing of the anus and damage to the rectum and beyond that results from fisting and "footing" is a primary reason why many homosexuals walk around in adult diapers (or colostomy bags.)
-Mwalimu Baruti.

If you are a parent of a homosexual son who told you that he let someone put their hand or arm up his anus, what would you do? Because according to statistics over 60% of homosexual males engage in the aforementioned activities. It's highly probable your son is among this group. Would you at least admit that fisting is not the actions of sane individuals and that your homosexual son needs help?

The anus was not designed for hands, feet, objects or gerbils to go inside. Why anyone would feel compelled to put live gerbils up their anus is inconceivable. However, during the 80's and early 90's this so called 'fetish' reached epidemic proportion. Many homosexual males derived pleasure from someone placing live rodents into their anuses. I'm sure the practice still remains since homosexuality and its many perversions still remain. Homosexuals failed at trying to convince a nauseated public that the gerbil incidents were a homosexual myth, but the number of homosexual males turning up at hospitals to get dead rodents removed from their anuses was irrefutable. If these are not the actions of perverse sexual disorder then what is exactly?

How and why is the insane actions of persons so obviously, deliberately and admittedly intent on defiling and abusing their bodies for short term gratification being so readily condoned, accepted and in some cases sanctioned (States obliteration of longstanding sodomy laws) by such a large portion of the population that consider themselves straight, normal or sane? Is it simply fear? Or does western culture still not know right from wrong? These perverse sex acts give homosexuals a temporary, primal rush of sexual gratification and pleasure which enhances a predatory disposition and leads to even greater barbaric perversions.

What's the difference between fisting and young White girls cutting themselves with knives and razors? Apparently one is acceptable behavior and the latter is considered a disorder. Why so? Is it because fisting is more in line with the homosexual agenda while the later form of self mutilation simply scares the hell out of soccer moms? Aren't they both forms of self mutilation?

If sex with animals(bestiality) and being choked to the point of almost dying to achieve greater sexual stimulation (asphyxiation) aren't sexual/mental disorders then deriving sexual pleasure from beating and hurting someone during sex(sadism) and deriving sexual pleasure from someone beating you up during sex(masochism) is simply normal European behavior. By not classifying all such perverse acts as abnormal and labeling it's participants in need of psychiatric help, we are celebrating their insanity.

A most curious observation

You may deodorize or use chemicals to disguise human excrement but it's still fesis; waste. No matter how you dress it up the rectum is still a holding area for your body's bowel movements. For a male to "swear off" women means he wants nothing to do with them sexually. For the homosexual male that also means he's rejecting a natural feminine scent in exchange for a male's natural masculine scent. In addition, he must force himself to become aroused by what the vast majority of us consider unpleasant odors. That said, the smell of human fesis must be acceptable if not enjoyable to the homosexual male. The odor induced from anal sex that the average person will find offensive, the male homosexual has trained or tricked his brain into believing that the smell of human waste is good or a necessary part of his sexual environment. The scent of male/female sexual intercourse is distinctly different from that of anal sex. It is a natural aphrodisiac. The male response to the female sex smell is so stimulating that some men do not wash their hands after sexual intercourse in favor of smelling the female scent on his fingers throughout the day. Yeah ladies I know; ewwww!

To suffer through or rationalize an intolerable odor for sexual gratification is not merely a challenge but a disorder. Most people want sex to be associated with something pleasant, memorable and relishable. How does an offensive odor qualify? If the male libido is stimulated by the scent of natural feminine juices then by contrast the homosexual male is stimulated by..... You get the idea.

When I was a child, I panicked whenever the toilet paper would tear while I was in the process of wiping my butt. Don't laugh; it's happened to you too. No matter how cool or sophisticated we think we are we've all had that moment. As adults we no longer panic we simply wash our hands. However, the thought of getting fesis on your fingers is still repulsive; but apparently not to the homosexual male. During anal sex fecal matter will most certainly get everywhere and on everything; every surface that is touched during and every hand that is touched afterwards (unless properly sanitized). As discussed on the previous pages how does a normal male come to like fecal matter on his penis, hands and face? Think about your own torn toilet paper incident and you already have your answer. Why is something abhorrent to us pleasant to the homosexual? It is not normal. Therefore it's abnormal, right? Hense the term mental/sexual disorder. You may not like it but this is reality. I had to go there in order to make you understand the depth of which sexual disorder will take you.

Cropophilia is defined as someone who derives enjoyment and sexual stimulation from human waste. According to Walter Langer in his book 'The mind of Adolf Hitler,' Hitler was a cropophile. He was a homosexual who liked and was aroused by human waste all over him.

49

Translation; he liked being urinated and defecated on for his sexual pleasure. Weather true, or the fabrication of 'Jewish' historians, what's the difference between liking a little fesis on you and a lot? No, I'm not comparing homosexuals to Adolph Hitler as someone is surely going to suggest. What I am alluding to however, is that if you consider Hitler's sexual behavior repugnant and deviant then you must reject all perversion with an equal amount of condemnation.

Culture is Behavior/ Culture Mimics Behavior

Culture: The behavior patterns, arts, beliefs, institutions, and all other products of human -   work and thought, especially as expressed in a particular community or period.

When England lowered the age of consensual sex between males to age sixteen, one could argue, Britain was anxious to see their sons sodomized like their forefathers; the Greeks. But one could also reasonably argue Britain was protecting its homosexuals from prosecution. How was this possible? Britain, like America is governed by a mobacracy (Ruled by a mob of people). Since homosexuality started with Europeans, perpetrated by Europeans, internalized, practiced, institutionalized, and legalized by Europeans, then its obvious homosexuality comes naturally to Europeans as an innate part of their culture.

If you think that a good idea spreads quickly within a culture, then you must admit that a bad idea can spread like wildfire; stupid jackass stunts, stocking caps, botox in the buttocks, tongue piercing, dumb dances, sagging pants, and thongs (okay, I liked the thongs.)But you get the idea. Culture often mimics the least competent, intellectual or creative people among us. Yet the most intellectual, competent and creative people can also become victims to culture.

Television reinforces the idea that women have it better these days and that it's better to be a woman in today's society. Mass media's social effects on Black culture are toxic at best. Sitcoms and dramas with positive Black images are scarce. After almost a century in Hollywood, television and movies still portray so called minorities as villains and clowns. Black males are the sidekick buffoons to White heroes. To a young White child this reinforces superiority and to a Black child, inferiority; something undesirable. The steady trend for decades has been the Black woman hero. Hollywood usually shows Black women as heroes fighting against the system and of course her abusive Black counterpart. The Black woman is seen as the strong, protector, provider and nurturer, while the Black man is the undesirable pimp, clown or villain.

Subconsciously the young Black child internalizes these images. We may call it entertainment to see Tyler Perry's Madea character strong, fearless, sassy, fighting and rescuing women while beating down and destroying Black men, but its not entertainment it programming. Go ask a 5, 6, or 7 year old Black boy or girl about Madea and the response is extremely positive. Then ask them about their own father; their excitement and enthusiasm wanes. The Black men who surround Madea are evil, lazy or womanizing wrong doers. As the child's mother cheers Madea on, she denigrates the child's father as a good for nothing looser or deadbeat. Who will the boy psychologically want to emulate? The man dressed as a woman who everybody loves and respects or his own father? Who will the Black girl hold resentment and fear towards? You get the point. A mother should always respect the father of her child when that child is around. This is but one example of social programming at its best. Homosexual ideas are being planted and fertilized.

One must also acknowledge that Black mothers who fear prison or death for their male children unconsciously effeminize them at an early age. They are overprotective to the point of blocking a young male's natural development. This very real fear derives from the historical attacks on Black males who stood up and died just for being a man. Once again we see a social construct that inhibits natural development. Historical documentation as well as comparative observation will show that homosexuality does not come naturally to Blacks. It was and still is being forced upon a culture still fighting an inferiority complex. Only now instead of a sword, psychology is the weapon of choice. Many schemes have been devised to link homosexuality to ancient Africa as a way to cultivate seeds of assimilation and precedence, but they've failed. In America, European culture and values are dominant and are always imposed upon other cultures.

When something does not come natural, our need for acceptance and compliance can make some of us work hard to prove that it is; even if it hurts. The Black male homosexual forcing his mind and body to become female when his D.N.A knows that it is male creates a sort of break from reality. Normal thought processing can go haywire. Think about a woman wearing tennis shoes for 25 years suddenly slipping into a pair of high heels, or a child trying to force a circle into a square peg. It doesn't work. Study the actions and mannerisms of many Black male homosexuals. Their attempts to mimic women are always exaggerated, ridiculous caricatures of how real women behave. In public, Black male homosexuals try so hard to convey the fact that they're homosexual that it's both amusing and frightening at the same time. By contrast and for the most part, the average White male that's homosexual cannot easily be detected until he says or does something to reveal himself. Rock Hudson was a perfect example of that.

Yet and still homosexuality and acting feminine has provided a safe haven for many scared Black males. They truly believe that White racists will no longer see them as a threat to White supremacy and allow them to go about their way confrontation free. They want to be viewed as fun-loving, non-political court jesters who can get along with everybody. They are wrong. A scared and confused Black male can put on a dress and play pretend games all day long, but he'll never be able to hide his black skin. They have continued to find racism lurking around every corner. Acting feminine and playing pretend games does not confront, alleviate or eliminate such a problem.

The number one reason why so called 'down-low' Black males and 'homo-thugs' are forced to cloak themselves among regular Black men is because Black culture has always rejected such unnatural perversions. Culture follows people wherever they go. When something as alien to Black culture as homosexuality is being forced and coerced, its victims will undoubtedly act absurd. All one need do is take a look at the Black male and female homosexuals in your community. With their over the top outfits, antics and comments, one would think them to be characters in some Hollywood movie. They are so uncomfortable cross dressing and changing their voices that they over compensate their shame with boisterous, animated behavior. This behavior also allows them to ward off many challengers to this homosexual persona because the average person doesn't want to make a seen or come across as intolerant. It's obvious they don't comprehend that one can be homosexual without acting like a fool. In contrast, White male and female homosexuals are never uncomfortable or awkward in this state because their genetic memory bank dates homosexuality back to the origins of Europeans/Caucasians themselves.

The Superiority and Inferiority Complex

….And their relevance to homosexual behaviors and attitudes in Black culture.

<u>Superior:</u> 1. High or higher in order, degree, rank, quality, or estimation 2. Situated above or over 3. Arrogant; haughty 4. Indifferent or immune

<u>Inferior:</u> 1. Low or lower in order, degree, rank, quality, or estimation 2. Situated under or beneath 3. Of little or less importance, value or merit 4. One lower than another; as in station or worth. Subordinate; underling.

<u>Complex:</u> 1. Intricate; complicated. 2. A group of repressed ideas and impulses that compel patterns of feelings and behavior.

"The darker races of mankind and the Black race in particular will keep the White race busy for the next 100 years in defending the interests of White Supremacy. The Black singer is coming with his song, the poet with his dreams, the sculptor with her conception of beauty and aw, and the scholar with his truth. The greatest marathon race of the ages is about to begin between the White race and the darker races of mankind. What Jack Johnson seeks to do to Jeffries in the roped arena will be the ambition of Negroes in every domain of human endeavor." –Rev. Reverdy Ransom on White Supremacy and an upcoming boxing match between Jack Johnson and Jim Jeffries

And after the Black champion Jack Johnson whipped the great White hope Jim Jeffries…

<u>A word to the Black man</u>: "Do not point your nose too high. Do not swell your chest too much. Do not boast too loudly. Do not be puffed up. Do not let your ambition be inordinate or take a wrong direction. Remember, you have done nothing at all. You are just the same member of society as you were last week. You are on no higher plane, deserve no new consideration, and will get none. No man will think a bit higher of you because your complexion is the same as that of the victor at Reno."
-Los Angeles Times, July 5, 1910

Jack Johnson's crushing victory over Jim Jeffries caused riots throughout all America; not just in the South. You have to realize Johnson didn't just publicly beat up a White man, but he openly beat down the White superiority complex within the psyches of White Americans; and he smiled the entire time.

Thoughts manifest words into being. If you're told that you're superior you'll act superior. If you're taught to believe you're inferior, you'll behave accordingly. When I say the words **'White Supremacy'** the first thing you think about is the Ku Klux Klan, white sheets, skin heads, Neo-Nazis and The Third Reich. But it's much more complicated then that. These words by their very utterance, evokes feelings of hate, fear, and helplessness; that usually leads to emotionally charged actions of violence, disrespect and immobility.

Although not physically locked inside a plantation, psychologically many Blacks have been bound since slavery. This is due to the inferiority complex; but the superiority complex was the key. You didn't have one without the other. What does a superiority complex have to do with homosexuality? People with a superiority complex do not value or respect other peoples culture or customs. In fact, they will unknowingly as well as overtly destroy it. People with an inferiority complex will not maintain or practice their own customs, culture or disciplines, but instead try to assimilate into a culture they feel is superior to their own. Many Blacks accept and champion homosexuality although it was never a part of their history, ancestry or spirit; because they know White America will laud, applaud and love them for it. They do not wish to fall out of favor with Whites. In fact, homosexuality was greatly shunned by ancient Africans and Native Americans when Europeans first brought its practice to their shores.

We know that the superiority/inferiority complex was created by the master to better control his slave, however, sense slavery, extreme emphasis has been placed on maintaining this lie. Before white children were of age to reason they were programmed to think their White skin was the 'end all and be all.' And to further that thinking their parents painted everything around them white; White's only eating facilities, water fountains, hospitals, buses, sports teams, schools, hotels, movie theatres, etc. They not only controlled the number of Blacks on the movie screen but the subservient, ignorant, buffoonery roles they could play. White folks across America saw these images and for generations and believed them to be true. It was through television, newspapers and magazines that these *White Supremacist* controlled the mental images White folks had of Blacks; creating the scared, lazy, watermelon and chicken eating stereo types that are still around today. By the time 'Tarzan' came along and for years saved White folks from Black cannibals, *'Birth of a Nation'* had irrevocably destroyed the image of Blacks and spurred lynchings, rapes, murders and vicious assaults of Black men, women and children across this country.

I like chicken and watermelon and so do most people. Can you imagine the power in making the entire nation think there was something wrong with people who ate chicken or watermelon? In actuality, there's something wrong with you if you don't like chicken or watermelon. Anyway, White supremacist passed the torch of hatred on to their children who kept this trend going with 'Step-n-Fetch it', 'Amos and Andy', and White men wearing Black paint on their faces and hands pretending to be Black and behaving like absolute idiots. Saturday morning cartoons rarely had Black characters and the programs that did, put them in minor or sub-servant roles. White children were able to see themselves as superheroes, doctors, lawyers, and adventurers while at the same time see Blacks as only able to point them in the direction of the trouble; allowing the White man to save the day.

When White children went to school every book was geared towards a *White Supremacist* doctrine. White children learned that Columbus discovered America, George Washington never told a lie, Custard was a hero, so called 'Indians' were blood thirsty and liked scalping White people, all their wars were righteous wars for a just cause, Christians were honest and holy, and to top it all off the teacher who was spewing all this nonsense was White just like them. This went on for decades. When integration started not only did Whites not want Blacks in their schools but now Black parents were forced to send their own children off to be educated by *White Supremacists*. And that still goes on to this day. Teachers, who know the truth, still teach distortions, half truths and lies to these impressionable minds.

In the meantime, White children sit inside a classroom and receive a totally different educational experience than Black children. I think it sad that school curriculums haven't deviated much over the years especially since it was Black, southern legislators who bought about the public school system and other social programs in the first place.(Reya 125) For so long school and public libraries offered very few books by or about Black people. The books Black children were forced to read spoke of White achievement and conquests and that Black achievement was practically non-existent. With the exceptions of Fredrick Douglass, Harriet Tubman, George Washington Carver, Booker T. Washington and Martin Luther King, Jr., this bias educational system kept Blacks in perpetual darkness and psychological slavery. Is it a question as to why Black children start out with a deficit and an inferiority complex?

This fictional doctrine of White superiority has been ingrained throughout every aspect of Western society. Walk into any bank, library, school, courthouse or public facility and you'll see huge portraits of White men decorating the walls. Every building, stadium, school, or ship has a White mans name on it. Whites take pride in seeing each other supervising jobs, controlling wages, dispensing pay checks, and in the ability to hire and fire Blacks at will. And every Friday when a White man walks into a bank to cash his check, as he looks down to count his money, he is further reminded of his assumed superiority by seeing the white faces on every dollar bill staring back at him. Would this not, even on a subconscious level, make one race feel superior to another?

By contrast, Black people see all the same images but it has the exact opposite effect; for instance the judicial system. A Black man can dial 911 during an emergency; a white voice will answer the phone, dispatch white cops, and make him stand before a white jury, as he gets sentenced by a white judge. God forbid if he was to become ill. He'd then have to depend on a White doctor to help him get better. That in of itself can leave the strongest Black man feeling powerless and inferior to the point were he must now alter his behavior to accommodate and survive in a White power structure.

Black and White children can aspire to be whatever they choose to be yet White children maintain a huge advantage. But what if someone told them both the truth? What if all schools disclosed the factual information that virtually everything in American society was invented, created or refined by a Black man; everything from the books they read, the shoes on their feet, the sugar in their cereal, the symbols on their money, and the religion they currently serve, was created by Black minds. Would that make a difference? I think so. Just by telling the truth Blacks would become less inferior and Whites would become less superior because the truth would set them both free. For example; the world knows that a Black man named Matthew Henson trekked through the ice and snow to be the first human being to set foot at the North Pole, yet White Americans lied in history books and said it was Robert Peary. Henson literally saved Peary's life on at least three separate occasions, making it possible for him to go on. We all know that Egypt is in Africa, yet Europeans dug the Suez Canal and tried to convince the world it's in the Middle East. Eli Whitney didn't invent the cotton gin but we'll never know the name of the slave who did. This is all geared towards the interest of White superiority. Fortunately, we do know the names of these other smart, innovative Black inventors:

Folding cabinet bed-Sara E. Good

The air conditioner-F.M. Jones

The refrigerator-John Standard

The lawn mower-John A. Burr

The Gas mask-Garrett Morgan

Refrigerated trucks and trains-Fredrick Jones

Lawn sprinkler-Joseph Smith

Street sweeper-Charles B. Brooks

Elevator-Alexander Miles

Automatic gear shift (automobiles)-Richard Spikes

Automatic air brakes-Grandville Woods

Shoes (lasting machine)-Jan Ernest Matzeliger

Train telegraph-Grandville Woods

Advanced printing press-W.A. Love

Letter box(mail box) G.E. Becket

Fire extinguisher-Thomas j. Martin

Ironing board-Sara Boon

Type writer-Lee Barrage

Blood banks-Charles Drew

Street lights-Lewis Latimer

Traffic signals–Garrett Morgan

Printing press-W.A. Lavalette

Pencil sharpener-John Love

Fountain pen-William Purvis

Reshaping machine(bread doe machine) – Joseph Lee
The 'car coupling'(train connecting device)-Andrew Beard
Automatic lubricating systems('the real McCoy')-Elijah McCoy
Agricultulural genius (dry coffee, paper, ink, plastic:
Hundreds of products from the peanut and
the sweet potato)-George Washington Carver
Arthritis and glaucoma medicine-Percy Julian
Postmarking & canceling machine-William Berry ?
The Guitar-R.F. Flemmings Jr.
Electric trolley-E.R. Robinson

Electric trolley-Albert Robinson
Mop-Thomas Stewart
Golf tee-G.F. Grant
Player piano-J.H. Dickerson
Comb-W.H. Sammons
Steam table-George Kelly
WaterCloset (toilet stool)-J.B. Rhodes
Corn silker-R.P. Scott
Railway signal-A.B. Blackburn

…..And the list goes on and on and on.

"To keep control of a people you must keep them ignorant of their accomplishments."
-Dr. Margaret G. Burroughs, Author, Historian & Lecturer

How different would Black school children be if they knew their cousins, uncles, aunts and grandparents practically invented everything we use in America today? The key to economic prosperity in this country was the patent. For decades it was against the law for Blacks to patent their inventions. Many were forced to get someone White to secure their patents, and that person would then turn around and steel their invention. Through reverse engineering, coercion, or theft a lot of White inventors and corporations were able to use the knowledge left by Black inventors to make a name for themselves and prosper; while never disclosing the true source of their so called accomplishments. With so much information with held, and so much propaganda being fed to the masses for so long, it comes as no surprise how Europeans began to think themselves superior while Africans began to view themselves as inferior. Throw religion into this equation and the Black mind was turned completely upside down. Racists made God and *White Supremacy* one and the same. It Okayed violence, injustice and murder. This religion came with pictures too; Jesus is White, therefore his father is White.

European religion forced upon Blacks was a political tool to make them more manageable, forgiving of and open to White oppression. Passed down by generation, these images helped to facilitate an internalized fear of Whites and created a boundary Black men, women, and children would dare not cross. And a lot of them are still afraid to cross it to this day. It only took a few years for Hitler to convince the entire country the '**Aryan'** was superior to the rest of the world. Imagine what generation after generation after generation of Black and White Americans have been programmed to believe about each other.

Many years ago the so called 'evil White people' wanted to treat their slaves <u>bad</u>. The so called 'decent White people' wanted slaves to be treated <u>good</u>. The slaves themselves wanted slavery to end altogether. And it's the same way today, politically and economically; a rigid cast system is maintained. Who's right? Who's left? Who's right? Who's wrong? The same perimeters of superiority have been passed down by generation. The inferiority complex is what causes Blacks to wish for integration into the troubling minds of disturbed thinking, rationalizations and behaviors. The good Whites will say "haven't we done all we could for you people; Why won't you accept homosexuality? We know what's best for you people."

In order to please and/or appease Whites many Blacks embrace homosexuality and its many tentacles of perversion. They fear any form of obstinacy or decent would bring down the wrath of those they've been programmed to view as superior, hence financial rewards would disappear and the monetary value they've placed on their lives would be threatened. They in essence accept homosexuality in exchange for their souls.

When you view anyone as being superior to yourself its easy for you to then internalize their ideas. No matter how insane the idea, your inferiority complex makes it seem logical; even prudent. In fact, some Negroes think that it is because they are inferior that they didn't come up with the idea themselves

Racism Disguised As Superiority

Since superior minds are suppose to emit superior ideas, why does homosexuality still thrive in the western culture? A so called 'superior mind' embracing homosexuality is like a NASCAR driver racing down a dead end street; neither one has a future. The problem with American history with all its false grandeur and embellishment is that it should simply be called White history. Because to accurately study and document America's history of failure, achievement and accomplishment, one would have to include everything of historic relevance that happened on American soil or elsewhere that affected American life. Rich Whites give poor Whites- Blacks as scapegoats as to why they're poor. This process keeps poor Whites blind to the reality that rich Whites are taking all of their money. Economic superiority propaganda is the foundation of western culture.

"Fear those that you cannot understand and hate what you fear."

Here's a perfect example of the superiority complex in action. During World War II, a time when Black and White Americans soldiers were supposed to be united, White American soldiers became enraged at Black GI's who were openly fraternizing with White European women. That's right; White English women began ignoring White GI's and were throwing themselves at Black soldiers as soon as they set foot in England.

White American males were so incensed it sparked race riots right there in England, in the middle of the war. Slavery and overt racism was banned in 1795 throughout England. But young, White, American soldiers took their hate and superiority complex with them around the globe. And since there was no 'Jim Crow' laws in England, American GI's tried to invent their own. Quite naturally the Black soldiers weren't going for it, so deadly riots broke out everywhere. After order was restored the White soldiers could only resort to running around telling European women that Black soldiers had animal tails in hopes of scaring them off. That didn't work either. It is pathetic what the superiority complex has done to the southern White male psyche. Yet another historical fact your teacher didn't tell you in history class.

Recently, White America's superiority complex ran ramped during the 2008 Barack Obama presidential campaign. A lot of supposed middle class Whites were among the many minorities who lost their homes during the 2008 foreclosure crisis. They were the many who ran out and got big houses to create and maintain the illusion of middle class status. Yet everyday they reported to work on the same low wage jobs next to the minorities they wanted to distance themselves from and thought themselves superior to.

This is a generational mind set. Years ago Erin Rhea observed the exact same patterns. "They were people who had middle class aspirations, but were generally insecure and often bitter because they did not obtain middle class rewards." (124) It sounds kind of like the comments that got then presidential candidate Obama into trouble when he talked about; certain whites 'clinging to guns and religion,' except he didn't include racism and a crumbling illusion of White superiority. In other words these were the people America's aristocracy pissed on their heads and convinced them it was raining. These are the people Bill and Hillary Clinton, John McCain, and Sarah Palin consider poor White trash. Yet these patriotic Americans will break their backs to serve them because they believe the aristocracy would include them in their success. As usual they were wrong. This exact delusional behavior was noted over 40 years ago.

"The second most numerous group in the United States....millions of persons who regard themselves as middle class and are under all the middle class anxieties and pressures, but often earn less money then unionized workers. As a result of these things they are often envious, filled with hatreds and are generally the chief recruits for any radical right, fascist or hate campaign against any group that is different or which refuses to conform to middle class values....made up of clerks, shopkeepers and a vast number of office workers in business, government, finance, and education, these tend to regard their white collar status as the chief value in life and live in an atmosphere of envy, pettiness, insecurity, and frustration. They form a major portion of the Republican party's supporters in towns of America, as they did for the Nazis in Germany thirty years ago."

-*Carroll Quigley*

They regard their white collar status (jobs) as their chief value in life. For them to lose their job would run them straight to the nearest hate monger to blame Blacks. For them to acknowledge that they are working class and not middle class, would shatter their illusion of superiority and is the equivalent of waking up a man who's been sleep walking. It is traumatic. For these people to vote for Obama was to acknowledge that they were wrong. That they in fact are not superior and that the White leaders they identified with had used them and sold them out. These Whites who lived the lie of superiority must now look into the face of a Black man to save what's left of their crummy lives. When they voted for Obama they were admitting that Blacks are not inferior and that they themselves were never superior and that class not race was their true enemy.

In overstanding (yeah, I said overstanding because this is too important to understand) the role inferiority still plays in the sub-conscious minds of millions of Blacks everyday, you'll see how it is forever tied to the superiority complex in Whites. How one group of people are made meek, fearful and hesitant to speak up, and the other group believe that whatever they say or do is right; even when it's wrong. People with a superiority complex do not like being challenged and look down on the opinions, criticisms and observations of those they've viewed as inferior. This complex is so ingrained in American culture that for the most part Blacks aren't even aware of its presence in their minds. This goes double for homosexual sex-styles, attitudes, compliance and the internalization of such ideas in the Black community. It is what brings Blacks to the steadfast defense of White culture instead of their own. Believe it or not, many Negroes have died defending White supremacy.

"When are we White Americans going to get over our ridiculous obsession with skin color …How long until we White people get over the demonic conviction that white skin makes us superior …How long before we White people get over our bitter resentment about being demoted to the status of equality with non-whites …How long before we get over our expectations that we should be at the head of the line merely because of our white skin..." -Andrew M. Manis, professor of history at Macon state College

Whether it's the right to vote or equal health care for all, many White Americans resist any progress geared towards non-whites because such laws chip away at their perceived superiority. It creates the traumatic effect that spawns hate groups and anti government movements. You'll often hear them speak in code; "we want our country back." These White supremacist groups are angry because Blacks are getting things they believe "they" should only be entitled to having. They no longer run around hidden beneath white sheets. They live on your street and work right next to you everyday.

Stockholm Syndrome

Wikipedia: Stockholm syndrome: is a <u>psychological</u> response sometimes seen in an abducted hostage, in which the hostage shows signs of loyalty to the hostage taker, regardless of the danger (or at least risk) in which they have been placed.

"Keep your captive happy so that you can stay alive."

On August 23rd, 1973, two men carrying machine guns entered a bank in Stockholm, Sweden. After shooting their guns into the air, Jan-Erik Olsson, a prison escapee, told the horrified bank employees "The party has just begun!" The two bank robbers held four hostages, three women and one man for 131 hours. The hostages were strapped with dynamite and held in a bank vault until rescued five days later. When the hostages were interviewed, it became clear that they actually supported their captors and actually feared the law enforcement agents who came to their rescue. The hostages had begun to feel that their captors were actually protecting them from the police. One woman later became engaged to one of the hostage takers and yet another developed a legal defense fund to assist with their defense fees. The former hostages were obviously suffering from what has now come to be known as **'Stockholm Syndrome.'**

When it comes to confronting Eurocentric behavior quite a few Black Americans who have been weaned within the confines of a hostile society have developed a strong case of Stockholm syndrome. To many Blacks it is absolutely frightening to even consider speaking out against homosexuality. And still to others, no matter how insane the action, 'White is right.' Waiting for so called minorities to challenge the status quo is the equivalent of waiting for a woman suffering from battered wife syndrome to stand up to her husband. There is little resistance from blacks when it comes to opposing homosexuality on the national stage because of the paralyzing fear of what those in charge may do.

For me to say that 'Blacks' are still oppressed in 2009, will undoubtedly draw eye rolls and hisses. White Americans think that because Obama is president, B.E.T. is still on the air, and O.J., Michael Jackson and R. Kelly didn't go to jail, times have changed. But any group of people who are battered, manipulated, jobless, abused and/or denied the ability to create and control their own economy, and in doing so their own destiny, is a group of oppressed people. Isn't oppression abuse?

So why do we love our abuser, America? Isn't that the $100,000 question? Just like the battered wife, we think we can change our abuser or that we somehow deserve his beatings. Many black folks do what they have always done; pray to Jesus and leave it in his hands, while they prepare their own children for yet another generation of physical and psychological abuse.

Do you remember watching the footage of Rodney King being assaulted and beaten after his police chase? To this day, many white Americans believe the police officers were within their rights and were simply doing their job. Theirs is a serious disconnect. After the four police officers were acquitted, life for white Americans proceeded as usual; but not for blacks. Throughout the country, their fear and hatred of police intensified. Tens of thousands of black mothers and fathers feared for the safety of their sons. Some took away their car keys while others imposed stricter curfews.

Now more then ever, Black parents constantly warn their children; "watch out for the man, dress this way, talk that way, keep your hands in plain sight, move slowly, don't argue with the police."
Long before there was a video camera to record white cops brutality beating on a Black man, the Black community was well aware of the problems it had with law enforcement. But to witness the white power structure, with the entire world watching, act in compliance by acquitting the four police officers was even more traumatizing. Imagine someone punching you in the stomach after you've just finished dinner; if you didn't throw up you probably wanted to.

The sad but true fact is that every since a police force was started in this country it did nothing but favor and cater to the White power structure and maintaining its control. During and immediately after slavery, law enforcement had been the antagonist of Black Americans. The resentment and forewarnings have been passed down among Black people from generation to generation to this very day. All the while being validated by police abuses every step of the way.

During what is commonly referred to as **'the second slavery'** Blackmon notes the rapes Of Black women who came to visit or bond their men out of jail throughout the South; men who were illegally kidnapped by the police.

"At the lumber camps in southern Alabama, women seeking the freedom of their men were simply arrested when they arrived, chained into their cells, and kept to serve the physical desires of the men running the camps. The 'slave' camps and mines produced scores of babies nearly all of them with White fathers." (*Slavery by another name, p.305*).

Now focus on what it truly means to 'keep your captive happy so that you can stay alive.' Then think about the Negroes at your place of employment. Some of them have and will do absolutely anything to stay in the good graces of their employer and keep that job; no matter how degrading the task or time consuming the chore. Fear and only fear is their primary motivation. The boss can treat them like crap yet they refuse to quit. For them to do otherwise is to be 'put to death' financially. And since there is no such thing as job security in European culture, that includes blacks and whites, Negroes will do anything to be noticed by their boss. It is not enough for them to be deemed successful by their own family and community; it is the validation and praise from their workplace abuser they value most. They go to extremes to keep their boss happy. Other blacks commonly refer to them as 'Uncle Toms' but that's a bit too gracious, especially since Harriet Beecher Stowe's Tom was righteous. Stockholm syndrome would be a more correct analysis.

Some years ago, I was hired by a company called BECO as an assistant superintendent of a residential construction project. I had been self-employed and out of the work force for quite a while when I initially applied for the position. I had no idea how much employer and employee relations had changed, or maybe it was I who had changed. But it was there where I encountered two Negroes that fell right out of an old **Step-n-Fetch- it** movie; **Lamont and Ivan Weller**. Ivan, the younger of the two, who preferred the nickname 'O', was always arguing with his brother Lamont about work assignments. Their arguments were always loud, ignorant and based on some petty disagreement. They'd worked at BECO for a few years and immediately resented my being hired at a higher pay rate and position than them.

Lamont did everything imaginable to cater to our boss, John Croft. Croft was a loud mouth, red-faced, diminutive man, who felt the need to overcompensate for his lack of stature or personality by being boisterous and pretending to know everything. One could find a John Croft on any construction site in America. European culture breeds them in abundance. No matter how disrespectful or mean-spirited our boss was towards him, Lamont Weller remained loyal and steadfast. Until now, I never understood why Lamont treated John Croft, an arrogant mental dwarf, who always smelled as if he'd just showered in cheap cologne, with such awe and reverence. Now I know it was the awful effects of the Stockholm syndrome. To say that Lamont loved and breathed any and everything that was European would be an understatement, for if they were to ever do an autopsy, they would find Lamont Weller's insides as white as David Duke's.

On the job, Lamont greeted every White man that crossed his path with the same happy, buck eyed, shiny teeth, shuck and jive expression that would make Amos and Andy proud. God knows it was simply disgusting to watch. On the other hand, he greeted and spoke to Blacks on the site with anger and a resentment that was absolute. "All the white guys on the job like me," he'd remind the Black employees weekly. Lamont needed 'White' approval in order to feel like 'a somebody.' I don't know if it was because they were from the small city of Emporium, where self respect is against the law or if John Croft had paid for him to attend obedience school, but Lamont's confusion ran deep and he clearly hated himself. His young sibling wasn't much better. His brother 'O' went out and impregnated the first 'White girl' he came across. And if she was to be the status symbol he needed to feel good about himself, he was in big trouble. She was described by his own brother Lamont as lazy and homely.

Anyway, "O" admitted to spending many hot summer nights around the house of Walter, a White carpenter whom "O" admired, and whom admitted to being bi-sexual (A term homosexuals use when they're ashamed of being called homosexual). In hindsight, I now understand why at times "O" exhibited such feminine qualities. He'd obviously spent one too many a night around the house of an admitted homosexual. Oh yes, Stockholm syndrome made brothers Lamont and Ivan Weller surrender their anus' (one figuratively, and the other literally) to the White boss' they feared and revered.

Needless to say, my awareness of self did not allow me to fit into this kind of power dynamic. After a number of stabs to John Croft's fragile ego, I was fired. I never saw Lamont or Ivan Weller again, but I'm sure that wherever they are, they're still bending over. And Lamont is still bootlicking and shuffling his way around construction sites. One day he'll die and fulfill his dream of going to a 'yes-sir' boss, Step-n-Fetch it, shiny teeth, buck-eyed, Uncle Tom heaven.

For generations, Africans were kidnapped and made to submit to European rulers. Even after being 'freed,' they received no money, therapy, guidance or counseling to help them get pass their gruesome ordeal. Unfortunately, they passed the torch of fear, anxiety and inferiority down to their children. For generations they've fed their children attrition, passivity, benevolence and forgiveness for 'sins' yet to be committed by their former master's children, while the children and great-grandchildren of slave masters are passed down superiority, arrogance and entitlement. And this cycle continues to this very day.

It is these Negroes who give loyalty to the more powerful abuser, in spite of the danger this loyalty puts the victim in. Exploitation, which in itself is abuse, always creates victims. To a serial abuser, victims are necessary to maintain an illusion of power and powerlessness amongst the abused. Victims of mass abuse can easily become disillusioned and be preyed upon over and over again. A vast majority of lifelong victims have no idea that they are in fact, victims.

People with Stockholm syndrome will most certainly justify their abuse. "If I hadn't of done this or that, he wouldn't have hit me," battered wives often chant while protecting the husband from angry family members. Psychologically rationalizing their abuse has made many Negroes join their abuser's causes. As a result, they commit vicious acts against each other in order to please and identify with their abuser. Powerless people often take their anger and frustration out on those who are even more powerless than them.

Do you remember the 14 year old Utah girl, Elizabeth Smart? She was kidnapped by a homeless, religious pervert and kept tied to a tree near their campground. After a couple of months, the kidnapper was able to take Elizabeth Smart out in public. They kept a veil over her face, but she no longer tried to escape. She even told people she was her abductor's 18 year old wife. I imagine after repeated rapes by the dirty, filthy, deranged 'holy man,' she actually believed that. After nine months and quite by coincidence, the police stumbled upon her. She still did not reveal her identity. In fact, it wasn't until the officers presented her with a picture of herself did she break down and admit who she was. That was Stockholm syndrome at its worst.

Let's be logical but honest about observing and analyzing twisted, cultural behavior. If you were to observe Black women running around with blond wigs or hairweave and blue contact lenses covering their eyeballs, one could easily conclude they are absolutely mad, crazy or insane. If you were to dare approach these women and ask them why they changed their appearance in such a way, they would probably say they just "wanted to try something different." Oddly enough, they didn't change into African braids, dreads or a dashiki, their change was more to relate, imitate or appeal to the European culture and hierarchy. They wanted to look like White women.

Quite naturally these are the Black women that feminist agitators love to place in positions of authority over Black men. Go to any shipyard, construction site or warehouse in America and you'll find ignorant, blond-haired, blue eyed Black women yelling, threatening, posturing and verbally abusing Black men; all under the guise of "I'm just doing my job." They have taken the place of the white male overseer, but instead of protecting the master's house, she is protecting his economic interests and doing so with very little training.

If homosexuality is alright with the abuser, then it is alright with the abused. If fear is what "makes the servant praise his master," then unfortunately we're going to see a lot more hostages turned into homosexuals.

EUROPEANS AND GOLD JEWELRY

No where else on earth was the effort to demonize, subjugate, and shatter the minds and bodies of Blacks than right here in America. As irony would have it, in as much as Whites tried to destroy Blacks, at the same time they wanted to poses their strength, their-disciplines, their unity, their dances, their music, their God and their very souls. That envy has endured for centuries. It preceded <u>collagen</u> injections in the lips to make them fuller, tanning salons to get darker and melanin pills; God knows what they're made of. From the moment the pedophile, rapist, murderer, kidnapper, liar, and Christian, known as Christopher Columbus, set foot in "New Europe," he couldn't take his eyes off the natives. In his log he describes them as beautiful, perfect and innocent, before he commenced to killing, kidnapping and corrupting them.

Jealousy is an internalization of a strong desire to covet something physically, emotionally or spiritually that we ourselves do not poses. For example; when Columbus and his band of mercenaries saw the natives wearing the very gold, silver and other precious metals they worshipped, they had to have it. When they saw how these coveted stones gleamed off these native's bodies, they had to get their hands on them. But when these Europeans put the gold and silver around their necks and wrists it didn't look or feel the same. And to this day Europeans are still trying to figure out why. It's simple; Whites lack the melanin to illuminate gold, silver, diamonds, rubies, onyx or any other precious stone. And that's not meant to be rude, mean spirited or unkind; just factual.

It is why most White folks don't even bother to wear jewelry. Go out and take a close look at Europeans that do decide to wear jewels. It doesn't do anything to enhance them or their aura. Then take a look at a Black person wearing a gold chain or even the most inexpensive piece of jewelry; it shines. And the darker the flesh the more the metals are illuminated. It's the reason why Europeans place such high value and emphasis on diamonds. Diamonds emit such a powerful glow that people often notice the diamond, focus on its monetary value and not the person wearing it. Although they are unable to activate the energy inside the stone, Europeans always want the biggest diamond they can find on their fingers, wrists or around their necks.

THE POLITICS OF DECEPTION

Homosexuality and God

"Suffer the little children to come unto me for theirs is the kingdom of heaven "- Matthew 19:14

I wonder how many Catholic priests quoted those verses before pulling down the pants of some eight year old boy and viciously sodomizing him. Since the number one cause of male homosexuality is adult homosexuals raping and molesting boys, and these boys grow into men who molest other boys, the Catholic church must be responsible for tens of thousands of homosexuals the world over. Catholic priests didn't just start molesting boys or any other child for that matter; they've been doing it for centuries. It's only been recently that the world decided to step up to the plate and go after them for this sickness. They've only recently began to face a small degree of accountability.

Since Greece and Rome are the birthplace of organized homosexual rapes, one could argue that Catholic priests were just doing what they've always done to young boys; that which comes naturally. However, I do find it funny that the Romans were renowned homosexuals who persecuted Christians, but now they're basically Christians pretending to chastise homosexuals. I guess the ladder was more financially expedient. I say chastising because few Catholic priests have been sent to prison for sex crimes. In most cases, victims and families are given civil compensation using the money of their congregations. In other words, the Catholic Church used the victim's own money to pay them off. Brilliant!

Years ago, whenever people would raise an eyebrow or create a stir about their children being raped by a priest; the hierarchy within the Catholic Church would simply send the predatory priest to another town where the parishioners had never heard of him. And then simply pay off the victim's family. In most cases the priest would molest boys from broken homes or impoverished communities where adults rarely asked questions. The church did not fire the priest, call the police, send the victim to therapy, or worn the public that there was a predator on the loose. To them, rampant homosexuality and rape was a mere inconvenience that came with the territory.

 In essence, if you study even briefly how Catholics handled their scandals, you'd find out that they did more to help the sick, perverted priests avoid prosecution and detection than for the traumatized, helpless victims that trusted them. Add to the fact that the Catholic Church denounces the use of condoms, even in A.I.D.S. infested communities, one could convincingly argue that the Catholic Church was in fact, "Pro

Gay", and only pretends to be otherwise.

Meanwhile, so many of you believed that the Roman Empire with its soldiers and chariots had fallen. When in fact, the homosexual Roman army had removed its armor and replaced it with the garments of catholic priests. They exchanged their chariots for bullet proof "pope mobiles" and SUV's. And it worked. Why use a sword to do physically what you can use the Bible to do mentally? Power and influence has a religious chokehold on the world. Like it or not, Catholics are the original Christians and all western religions that prosper today had their start within those walls; including yours.

So what's going on? How did Catholics get this way? Do your research; the Catholic Church has been jaded since its conception. The Catholic Church fought the crusades to hide its origins and truths about Christianity from the world. "The Church of Rome defended by violence the empire which she had acquired by fraud". –Edward Gibbon.

In 306 A.D. Emperor Constantine ascended to the vacant throne and took over the then small, Jesus Christ occult, he made Christianity the "official" religion of the world and outlawed all other gods and religions. This decree was punishable by death. And Constantine was more than just zealous in his cause. Constantine eventually murdered his wife, son, brother-in-law, and strangled to death his own mother for not accepting this new "Christian" religion. To exalt the status of his new "CHRIST GOD", he then burned people, churches, houses, and thousands of books that revealed the origins of Christianity in an effort to stamp out any light of truth. And what was this truth, this fragile secret that thousands and thousands of men, women and children had to die for? That the basis of Christianity, the great lie was a made up story stolen many years earlier from the people in the land of Kemet (Egypt). Those thieves were called "Hyksos", "The Children of Israel", according to the historian Josephus. This invasion of Egypt in 1720 B.C. was ruthless and aimed at nothing less than the extermination of the Egyptian people and their replacement by the so called 'Israelites'.

The important point here is that Semites poured into Egypt following its conquest by fellow tribesmen. Before the invasion, thousands of Semites were allowed to live on the borders and raise families under the protection of Egyptian rulers. And how did the Jews repay them; with disloyalty and treachery. The first major betrayal of any group of peoples was the 'Jews' betrayal of African-Egyptians. Barbarians assisted by the people we call 'Jewish' today, betrayed the African rulers, then became the clerks and scribes to this illiterate group of goat herders. These Hyksos [children of Israel] power was broken during the eighteenth dynasty by Pharaoh Ahmes who drove these foreigners out of his land. These Jews took everything they'd learned in Egypt with them to Palestine and beyond. This is where African theology was stolen and placed into Jewish biblical reality. These 'Jews' had been in Egypt long enough to study and steal every "religious" concept these Africans had developed. This theology was then reworked and translated by Greeks and other Europeans.

World renowned Jewish psychiatrist Sigmund Freud (a.k.a. Sick man Fraud) agrees. Freud spent over 20 years researching the origins of Judaism, and by extension Christianity. He first wanted to know who was Moses and where did he come from. In his book 'Moses and Monotheism' Freud concluded that Moses was an Egyptian and the religion he gave to the Hebrew (Jewish) people was one of the Egyptian religion. In other words he gave them something that already existed. In fact, the name Moses is an African name. That's why his Ten Commandments sounded so familiar to anyone who ever bothered to do their homework. And although there really was no Moses this lie has been perpetuated for centuries. But what's more interesting is that the Jews themselves slipped up and told us that exact same thing in **Acts 7: 22**- 'Moses taught his people all the religious concepts he learned growing up in Egypt.' How much more evidence does one need before facing the fact they've been lied to? The reason why the Ten Commandments sound so familiar is because they are stolen passages lifted directly from what Europeans call "The Egyptian book of the Dead" **(The book of coming forth by day)** as well as great names like Moses; Mises was the great lawgiver in Egypt. The story of Jesus, which is actually the story of Horus, and Isis (Mary), Set (Satan) and so on.

By the time the most famous homosexual of all, King James came along, the Jesus Christ occult had long since taken root across the land. In 1601 King James gathered forty men to translate, rewrite, and bind together what we've come to know today as the King James Bible. These translators borrowed and stole every story, antidote, fable, and lie they had ever heard in order to complete this arduous task. Never mind the fact that a deity named <u>Krishna,</u> hundreds of years before Jesus Christ, was born of a virgin, performed miracles, had 12 disciples, died and rose again three days later; sound familiar?

Then of course there's <u>Buddha,</u> who was born of a virgin, performed miracles and was so holy that a slit had to cut in his mother Mira's side to pull him through; thus avoiding the impurity of the birth canal and all that icky afterbirth. Then there's <u>Mithra</u> and <u>Adonis,</u> both virgin born deities who preceded Jesus Christ by centuries. Which poses the question; how many sons did God have? How many virgins did he impregnate? Apparently dozens before Jesus Christ. The New Testament was written and altered under strict orders from King James to reflect the prophecies of the Old Testament coming to pass. That explains why a book that is supposed to be God's word is filled with so many errors, inconsistencies, plagiarism, and outright lies; God had no part in it.

I looked up Persius, Plutarch, Hermogones and other historians who lived around the same time as Jesus Christ or soon after, none of them document his existence.

Don't get me wrong, I like some of the Bible stories of heroism and diligence because I like good fiction writing; who doesn't? One of my favorite Bible stories was the one about Noah and the Ark. But after I found out it was taken from an ancient poem called, "The Epic of Gilgamesh" which itself was stolen from a hieroglyph of the Egyptian god 'Hathor' flooding the earth with her menstrual blood, I was upset. I hate plagiarists. Then of course there's Moses whose name was taken directly from Mises of Egypt and whose baby in a basket story was stolen from "Sargon's Birth"; more disappointment. After further research, I found that <u>afterlife, resurrection, circumcision, communion, Immaculate Conception, Christmas, Ten Commandments, Ark of the Covenant, holy trinity, Passover, judgment, flood, saviors, Easter, virgin birth, anointing</u>, etc., all came from Egyptian theology. Even the Christian ritual of baptism was stolen directly from the African-Egyptian who by emulating a baby coming new into the world from the water of its mother's womb, they submerged a man beneath water giving him a rebirth into the world; hence baptism. A thousand years before any similar concept appeared anywhere on earth, African-Egyptians believed in the afterlife which yielded rewards dependant upon sacrifice and tribute in this life.

Let's not forget the Torah and the Qur'an. Both relied heavily on the same stolen ideology. I must note however, that Islam is rooted in principle, where Christianity is entirely based on faith. That is the stark contrast in methodology. Islam, right or wrong is fundamentally uncompromising and has a visceral core belief in heterosexuality and the longstanding principles of "do unto others as you will have them do unto you." But, as a political tool in the hands of a few, Islam has been more than effective.

These so called 'holy books' that men kill for and women die for, and this beast called 'religion' was the fabricated hoax of the ages. Politics is religion. And homosexuals had a huge role in the politics of religion. Homosexual leaders of yesterday politicized religion as a means to psychologically control the masses with the same old "do as I say, and not as I do" attitude. Whether it was Pope Benedict IX, Constantine, or King James, the hierarchy of organized religion had a love/hate relationship with homosexuality. Religion has never stopped homosexuals because secretly; most high level religious leaders were and are still homosexuals.

[King James] was the irritating type of homosexual who insisted on promiscuous public embraces directed to any attractive young man in his court. James often acted with the bitchy spitefulness characteristic of his type of homosexuality; therefore, afraid to assert himself over any major crimes or abuses, he would pursue small offenders with hysterical savagery (Terrence McLaughlin; Dirt, NY Dorsett Press, 1971 pages 70-71)

King James would have words with women in his court over men. He was the equivalent of a psychopath who killed most of his sex partners when he was done with them. Like most homosexuals who hate to hear criticism, constructive or otherwise, James Stewart (King James) put his own mother to death so that he wouldn't have to hear her mouth. Why in God's name would God name his holy of holy books after a psychopath with a sexual disorder? Yet, this is the book Christians worship.

Every Sunday, sometimes Saturday and for many others, all day long everyday, millions and millions of Africans around the world invoke a homosexual ancestor of the Europeans. Today's most popular version of the bible was authorized by, approved by, and named for King James, a homosexual in 1604.... As interpreted for us by the Ancients, speaking is thinking, it is invocation, it is procreation, and it continues and extends culture. So, every time we say "the King James Version" his spirit is invoked. We invoke a European male who was a known murderer and homosexual. We give him power. -MWalimu Baruti, "Homosexuality and the Effeminization of Afrikan Males" Page 256. [Italics mine.]

"Christ had his John, and I have my sweet George" -**King James said in defense of his homosexual relationship to George Villiers, the Duke of Buckingham.**

In *Same-Sex Unions in Pre-modern Europe,* by John Boswell, the author details that during the middle ages same sex unions between males were a normal function within the Christian church; especially its hierarchy. The Catholic Church recognized and blessed such homosexual unions as Serge, Bacchus and Basil I. Popes John XII and Benedict IX held homosexual orgies inside the papal palace. Once again you must acknowledge that since these are the origins of the Christian church there's nothing holy about any of these characters. That's why I stated earlier; homosexuality and Christianity are joined at the hip. Still, this is the religion that you serve.

In every society for centuries a god has reflected its people. For example, in Ancient Greece as it's called, their gods were homosexual, rapist like them. They proudly wrote about it in Greek mythology, art and literature. Throughout the world the picture of God looks like the head of that particular culture and household. However, in Black American households God is in the image of a European. In fact, hundreds of Black churches still have pictures of a White Jesus deity hanging behind its pulpits. Nowhere on earth will you find a "Black Jesus" openly displayed in a White church. However, in private the Catholic Pope and his hierarchy worship and pray to a Black Madonna hidden beneath the bowels of the Vatican; interesting.

Western Christians laugh at Mid-Eastern Muslims who blow themselves up carrying out jihad, expecting twenty- one virgins and whine when they get to heaven. With twenty-one virgins someone's bound to get pregnant. Muslim men must be glad there is misogyny in the afterlife. This is indeed a man's version of heaven. What about women? Are there twenty one male virgins waiting to have sex with her? Don't laugh, that's no more ridiculous then your Christian belief in a mansion and streets of gold in heaven. The Bible is strict when it comes to sex on earth, but sex in heaven seems to be non-existent; angels without sex organs and God, living with his son up in heaven without a wife or goddess. Once again, it's a Chauvinistic, poor mans idea of heaven. Such thinking down grades God to a materialistic entity who wants you to be materialistic too. Man worships gold here on earth, but it would be of no significant value in heaven. What does a spirit need with a mansion or sleep?

I am not against "earthly riches" at all; however, unlike your pastor, I'm not claiming to be a conduit to God, a servant of God, a prophet of God, nor do I collect money from people who come to me looking for God. Women make up the bulk of these religious organizations, placing more time and effort into them than in their own families. The world pretends to despise the men who pimp, control, and traffic the flesh of vulnerable women, yet adore the men who pimp, control and traffic the spirits of vulnerable women. A woman being sold a dream, whether it's here on earth or in the afterlife, by a fast talking bottom feeder or an educated spiritual predator is equally despicable.

I think back to when Black churches were the firewall against homosexuality, and tried to help homosexuals. Now, like every other institution or organization in America, they've caved in to homosexual political pressure. It was the last ethical leg they had to stand on. They'd already Europeanized and capitalized all other aspects of their religious doctrine. That's absolutely mind boggling considering the Black church was created for protest and creative resistance. Those old slave, gospel songs; "Going up yonder", "God's going to trouble the waters", and "swing low sweet chariot" were creative resistance to oppression.

Once again, let's talk about facts instead of fiction, distortions, and lies. In 1680, the queen of Spain mandated all of the governors in the colonies to teach their slaves Christianity and proclaim Jesus as their Lord and Savior. And why would a master want to give a slave his god? They said that Christianity would make slaves more duty conscious towards their masters and perform these duties with absolute fidelity. And it worked. Black Christians are still performing these duties today. So, obviously they weren't Christians before they were slaves. Of course, slaves on plantations turned it into their own "Africanization of Christianity" as Dr. Ray Hagans calls it. I remember watching the movie, **"Goodbye Uncle Tom"** (Banned in America for obvious reasons) and seeing the depiction of how the early slaves fused ancestral tradition with Christian doctrine. That's why in today's Black churches we have so many people doing the holy dance, speaking in tongues, and have absolutely no idea why.

As vexed as I was throughout the movie, I was absolutely enraged at the so called "Holy Bibles" views and lies attributed to God concerning slavery. Take a look at **1 Timothy 6:1**, Paul tells slaves; if your master is a Christian they should; ….. **"Work all the harder because you are helping another believer by your efforts"**, or how about **1Peter 2:18**; **"You who are slaves must accept authority of your masters. Do whatever they tell you…..even if they are harsh. For God is pleased with you when….. You patiently endure unfair treatment"**. Saint Peter (as Catholics call him) goes on to say that **"if you suffer from doing right and are patient beneath the blows, God is pleased with you"**. Jesus Christ, what is this nonsense? Here's a good one from **Ephesians 6:5 "Slaves, obey your earthly masters with deep respect and fear. Serve them as you would serve Christ"**…….say what? If this does not reek of social and political control, then I don't know what does. Early American churches used those same verses to psychologically control their slaves and after slavery to control "Negro" populations. The idea the Bible puts forth, that God condones and is even pleased with slavery, makes me want to vomit. Of course, free thinking slave Nat Turner interpreted the Bible a bit differently and then went house to house killing 'Christians'. His crusade however, wasn't sanctioned by the church so he was caught and hanged. After that, reading was banned and punishable by death. That included the Bible.

After reading about how Jewish scribes and writers told us via the 'Holy Bible' how God Almighty feels about slaves and masters, I found it interesting that Jews despise Hitler. Adolph Hitler, a Christian by the way, declared himself master over all he surveyed and that included the Jews. In their Bible they tell us to honor and respect our Master yet they didn't, go figure. Do you still think the Bible is a credible tool against homosexuality? After reading the Bible cover to cover one would conclude that God was a self absorbed, Semite supremacist who loved Jews, hated gentiles and got upset every time a woman came on her period. Yet, it is the most beloved book in the world; unbelievable!

I was always taught that the Bible was God's word; a perfect book. I was taught that it should always be obeyed, respected, accepted, and applied to our lives. Yet, when you discover so many mistakes, falsifications and outright lies within this book, how can any sane person take it all seriously?

"Since many of those who have written about the war waged by the Jews against the Romans-a major historical event-were not there but write speculative, inconsistent, and meretricious(deceptive) *accounts from hearsay, while others were there but give false account, either because they are toadying to the Romans or because they hate the Jews, and their versions contain rhetorical praise and blame but not a trace of historical accuracy, I have decided to translate my history into Greek for the subjects of the Roman empire, since I myself fought against the Romans."*

- From Josephus' Jewish Wars.

A side bar to our study

January 14, 1991- Time Magazine article states: "Judaism is a horrible religion with racist origins that in principle should not exist at all." Two paragraphs ago I bought up Hitler and I got to thinking…. **Ezra 9:2** *Says 'Jews are the holy race and must not be polluted by mixed marriage'*. Didn't the Third Reich say the exact same thing? Could Hitler have been reading the Bible? Naturally, Adolph Hitler wasn't going for that. There can't be two master races. Hitler had already been in Egypt and other parts of Africa committing genocide. He'd read the sacred scrolls. He knew the facts about the true origins of the Bible God's so called 'chosen people' had written and it enraged him. What Hitler and his cronies did was inexcusable, but did Jewish racism lead to German racism? Was Hitler really the mad-man history made him out to be?

Maybe Hitler had read the Jewish Encyclopedia pp. 620-623 under "Gentile" which says **'a Gentile is like a beast and had less rights in a Jewish court then an animal'**, Or maybe the part that says **'the best among Gentiles deserves to be killed'**. How about **'Gentiles observing the Sabbath deserves death'**. Wasn't the Third Reich Gentiles? It further says **'Jews are exalted beings deserved to be praised.'** The Jewish TALMUD calls Jesus' mother a whore and Jesus a bastard. They call Jesus an enemy of Judaism and say that Jesus is in hell being burned with boiling hot excrement' (fesis). Jews controlled German banks and filled the ranks of the Bolshevik army that murdered the Romanov family. Did Hitler think his government was next? What if the Third Reich got their hands on a copy of the ZOHAR which says **'anyone who isn't Jewish wasn't a living soul'?** (ZOHAR,Bereshith 25 b). I imagine that wouldn't sit too well.

The Jewish TALMUD,Kethubath 11 b says **it's okay to 'have sex with 3 year old girls because they are young and their vagina's will close back up'**. I guess the writer spoke from experience. They also advocated **sex with little boys** as well. Today, these books and their foul, despicable, racist writings are hidden away, and only the Jewish hierarchy is allowed access to them. But this is the foundation of Judaism, hence part of the origins of the **Torah** and **Holy Bible**. Keep in mind the Jews said all of the above came with blessings from God. What do you think?

The New York Times October 29, 1996 article boldly states *European descendant Jews are counterfeits and have no bloodline to Abraham*. What? The most prestigious paper in the world wrote an article like that and they're still in business? They didn't have to print a retraction or settle lawsuits? I wonder why? Could it be that people are finally finding out the truth….finally reading the Bible for themselves instead of letting the pastor tell them what's inside? Why did it take so long for the lies of King James and his cronies to come to light? **The Dead Sea Scrolls** were discovered in caves many years ago. The Israeli government took hold of them and has since refused to let the rest of the world examine the ancient texts. What information are they hiding from us? Why can't we all share something that was meant for everyone? Because the Israeli government fears that once the world views these scrolls the truth about Judao-Christianity will be exposed forever.

Now, as your pastor would say; turn with me in your Bible to **Matthew 1:16**. It clearly states that Jacob was the father of Joseph which made him the grandfather of Jesus Christ. But, when I turned to **Luke 3:23** it says a fellow by the name of Heli was Jesus' grandfather. What the hell? I remember my pastor telling me that the Bible lists first born sons and heirs first, before anybody, so who could have made such a colossal mistake in this holiest of books? Let's examine a few more errors and inconsistencies.

The hate filled **Ezekiel in chapter 28:13** says Adam and Eve had fine clothes and jewels in the Garden of Eden. Was he high? Genesis clearly says they're naked. **Amos 4:11** said the people who survived Sodom and Gomorrah were like half burnt sticks. He must have been drinking some of Noah's fermented wine or simply didn't bother to read Genesis either. Check out **Genesis 7:17** which says the flood prevailed forty days but verse 24 says 150 days. **Genesis 8:13** says Noah was 601 years old when the flood came and died 350 years later at 950 years of age, but shouldn't he'd been 951 years old?

Turn to **Genesis 4:18** which says Enoch's first born son was Irad but in **Genesis 5:21** it says that Enoch's first born son was Methuselah. **Matthew 1:6** says David's first born son was Solomon, but when I turn to **Luke 3:32** it says Nathan was the son of David. This is important because they're claiming to establish Jesus' bloodline; however, Jesus could not have been the descendant of both men. In **Samuel 3:2** David's oldest son was Amnon. Although clearly not the oldest, Solomon was named so that he could be linked to the Jesus Christ bloodline. The five books of Moses refer to Pharaoh 155 times but never calls one by name. Why is it that the vast piles of Egyptian records say nothing about the Israelites, the oppression, the exodus, or Moses? The Egyptians were known for keeping detailed accounts of rulers yet **2 Kings 17:4** and **Jeremiah 44:30** name Pharaoh's that aren't found anywhere in Egyptian history. Why, because they never existed.

Genesis 1:27 says God created people in his own image…. God patterned them after himself; male and female he created them. But, **Genesis 2:7** says that God formed the man's body from the dust of the ground. **Genesis 2:22** says God made woman from Adams rib. **Genesis 1 and 2** clearly contain two separate creation stories written by two separate authors. Neither of which were Moses. Moses, by the way, wasn't there when

God said "let there be light", so how was he able to write down what happened? And, if he did write the first five books of the bible, how did he write about his own death in **Deuteronomy 34?** The remains of Dozens of African Pharaohs dating back over five-thousand years can be found in Egypt, yet the remains of not one man, woman or child mentioned in the bible can be found anywhere on this earth; especially Jesus. Why, because they never existed.

During the trial of Jesus Christ by Pilot, not one leper or blind man came to testify on his behalf. Jesus raised the dead, healed the blind, cripple and crazy in that very town yet strangely enough, no one person came forward to say a word in his defense. **Matthew 27:32, Mark 15:21** and **Luke 23:26** say that Simon carried Jesus' cross, however, **John 19:16** says Jesus carried his own cross. Who's right? Of course, all four gospels were written many years after Jesus' supposed death; therefore, the four gospels would not be an eye witness account but second, third and fourth hand information; hearsay.

"The Holy Bible" makes reference to over a dozen lost books. I'm not talking about the Gnostic gospels of Judas, Mary, Thomas etc., but the missing books someone wanted included among the 66 that we have. These books are mentioned in the Bible itself because someone expected them to be there. Where are they and why were they removed? What bit of information did these books contain that Jewish scholars didn't want us to see?   Where is The Book of the Acts of Solomon, **1 Kings 11: 14,** The Book of the Wars of the Lord, **Numbers 21:14,** The book of Jasher **Joshua 10:13** and all the books referenced in **1 Chronicles 29:29** and **2 Chronicles 9:29?**

The Gnostic gospels have been around for centuries. The book of Judas warns readers to stay away from the God of the Old Testament; however, it's still the same God in the New Testament, only now they've given him a son. The Gnostic gospels take a metaphysical approach to scripture and not the literal. That's why they were excluded from the sixty-six books we have today. In **Genesis 4:21** the Bible says that a Jewish man by the name of Jubal was the first musician –the inventor of the harp and flute. However, the Twa and other Africans are depicted on statues and monuments throughout Egypt playing a number of musical instruments; thousands of years before the Bible was written. How is that?

In **Leviticus 15:1** the Lord said to Moses, **"Give these further instructions to the Israelites..."** and goes on to say that he (God) wants women to bring him two turtledoves or two young pigeons as a burnt sin offering to make atonement for their menstrual cycle. Wow! In Genesis God created woman and made her perfect but by the time he gets to Leviticus he wants atonement for the normal menstrual cycle he gave her in the first place. How ridiculous is that?

Another example of how the gospels differ on important events.
Here's how the big four documented events following Jesus' resurrection.

Matthew 28:9	Luke 24:39	John 20:17	Poor Mark
They ran up and touched Jesus after his resurrection	Jesus told them to touch him	Jesus says don't touch me for I have not yet ascended to my father	Doesn't know what the hell happened

But, perhaps the most telling of all lies is in the gospel of Mark. The book of **Mark** stops at **Chapter 16 verse 8**. In fact, the footnotes at the bottom of my Bible states the remainder of Mark's writings was lost forever. However, magically verses 9-20 appear in everyone's Bibles. The footnotes say an anonymous person added those centuries later. And, to add insult to injury, they print verses 15-18 in red ink and say they were the last words of Jesus Christ. Unconscionable isn't it? Made-up folklore or not, nowhere in the Bible does Jesus say he's God, yet he is worshipped. Nowhere in the Bible does Jesus say he died for our sins; yet this is what we are taught.

I could continue for several more pages detailing and exposing the improbability, distortions, and lies of this so-called Holy Bible, but by now you get my point. Your reaction to these revelations may be cynicism or anger towards me or *possibly* towards yourself for being so gullible. But this type of programming and indoctrination began at birth. The **formulation** of our views and **belief system** started when we were children. And no, I'm not anti-Semitic (although no one has ever clearly or publicly defined what Semitic is) because the facts I just stated are public records we've either chosen or been taught to ignore.

"Religion can never reform mankind because religion is slavery?"
-Robert G. Ingersoll

Religions primary and strategic attacks are on the young. Our young children present an endless wealth of possibilities when it comes to religious exploitation. They provide earnest, sincere, free labor in the form of recruitment assignments; happily raising money by **soliciting** in the streets or door to door. They provide non-profit churches with a face of **pity** and **hope** that requires immediate, non-stop cash flow from a sympathetic public. Sadly, young minds are unable to ward off attacks from sexually repressed priests, choir directors, deacons, elders, and other congregants who approach them in the name of the Lord.

The psychology behind adults teaching children to believe they will burn in hell for the minutest transgression is without question mental abuse and trauma. The threat of hells fire squashes free thinking and limits constructive criticism. When children ask questions they deserve plausible, rational, verifiable answers; not abstract phrases or unsubstantiated folklore and certainly not indoctrination. Christianity has and will always put constraints on education outside of religious doctrine. Pastors and priests greatest fear is that a child may pick up a book other then the Bible. Once a child reads other books with saved historical documentation, credible information, and verifiable sources, the Bibles credibility becomes suspect to the child's reasoning. The developing mind of a child is always questioning everything; seeking out more answers to new questions. And since one door always leads to another, Christians fear that their Jesus Christ hold on the child will be severed. Therefore, the early years in your child's development is crucial to the Christian hierarchy who needs to instill the *dogma* and **fear** of hell's fire inside your little one. Why buy stock in any religion that would terrorize your child?

Yet and still, teaching a child that their pastors, ministers, reverends, priests and bishops are conduits to God and must be trusted, sets them up as marks for the most vile pedophiles. Christian adults who prey on children use their religious doctrine and a child's sense of loyalty to their faith to gain entry into their bodies. Parents who are afraid to talk to their children about the world outside the church, especially issues of a sexual nature, will leave it up to this false religious doctrine to keep their children's legs closed and zippers fastened. A homosexual Christian is no different from a homosexual. The perverse acts of the flesh come first, and then they confess to Jesus after the deed has been done. Once again negating any personal responsibility and escaping justice.

The dark ages, the Crusades, the inquisitions, most wars, diseases, tortures, murders and **rapes** committed around the world have always been committed by *Christians*. A majority of the **lynching** that took place in the South were done by *Christians* before or after church service. The **Oklahoma City bomber** and the guy who put **Anthrax in your mail** were both *Christians*. **A.I.D.S.** was created and disseminated by *Christians.* There is the inherent idea that Jesus will wash away their sins again and again no matter how many times they are committed. This negates any personal responsibility or accountability. The term Christian is simply an anagram to make people turn the other cheek. It is meant to disarm you and make you drop your guard. Terrorizing children to make them obey is nothing new. There is an old saying that if you school a child for the first seven years of his life, you ultimately set the pace for what he'll do for the rest of his life. It is the foundation of the psychosis for indoctrination.

When you step into your church and read and reiterate lies, how does that help you? False spirituality only decreases your spirit. Why go to church looking for magic and miracles? Examine your church, your pastor, priest, Rabbi and your Bible, Torah and Qu'ran; and why you really believe in them. Is it because your mother believed in them? A religious belief is a belief, not a fact. Has this three-thousand year old belief system made the world better or worse? Has communion, tradition, dogma, and symbolism made you God-like? Religion removes reality. Religious doctrine separates people from true spirituality, nature and the higher power. Our Creator deserves better than that.

There are churches on every block yet I see hungry people on every other corner. There are probably a hundred churches for every one soup kitchen; a hundred cathedrals and synagogues for every one homeless shelter. With so many Christians and so many resources why should any child go to bed hungry? But they do and their cries are heard around the world. Their prayers to Jesus consistently go unanswered. And his self righteous followers are blissfully deaf and blind. These are the Christians; out to build bigger and more extravagant churches. Every week they pile into these buildings like mindless sheep singing songs of praise to a man that never existed, while reading from a book that's deniable, unverifiable, and certainly unexplainable. Monday through Saturday their lavish buildings sit empty when they could be daycares, youth workshops and learning centers. This is Christianity and these are the Christians.

"The Christian religion is a parody on the worship of the Sun, in which they put a man called Christ in the place of the Sun, and pay him the adoration originally paid to the Sun." - Thomas Paine

This chapter was not meant to hurt or cause pain. But we must be scholastically correct when researching the truth. Like it or not, Christianity is not based on truth!

Homosexuality and the Bible

Christians use the Bible and Jesus as a tool against homosexuality because they lack the knowledge or research to engage in worthwhile debate. So they simply resort to quoting scripture and predicting hell's fire. What if a doctor went to medical school and was taught medicine from a two-thousand year old medical book; what diseases could he possibly cure? What use could he be to you today? It is the same with your Bible. The simple but sad fact is that most Christians refuse to investigate anything beyond the borders of their religion, therefore they never think outside the box and outside of the Bible. Our entire population must learn to take the Bible out of any arguments against homosexuality because it rarely works.

On **Monday, November 10, 2008,** I was thumbing through '*The Virginia Pilot*' newspaper and I came across Cal Thomas' column. His take on the so-called religious right and Evangelicals was interesting:

"Thirty years of trying to use government to stop abortion, preserve opposite-sex marriage, improve television and movie content and transform culture into the conservative Evangelical image has failed. The question now becomes: Should conservative Christians redouble their efforts contributing more millions to radio and TV preachers and activists, or would they be wise to try something else? I opt for trying something else."

Me too; my point exactly! It was ironic or calculated however, that just above his column was a piece concerning the defeat of 'Proposition 8' in California in support of gay marriage. These so called Evangelicals should examine the history and the foundation of the institution they serve. Read Job 14: 4 and work towards changing the environment that creates homosexuals. No man/woman can enter the spiritual realm by physical means. And you sure as hell can't fight a homosexual spirit by invoking a homosexual spirit, false doctrine, and a non-existent Jesus.

Religion as an institution, and Christians when it comes to issues of morality, has no credibility whatsoever. Their rhetoric promptly turns homosexuals and non-Christians away. And the Christian Bible is even less credible. False doctrine cannot free you it can only subdue you. The Bible is comprised of stories about Africans, stolen by Jews, controlled by Europeans, regulated by the powerful, obeyed by fanatics and believed by fools. It is the psychological tool that has for centuries kept this entire world in a perpetual hell.

How many programs has your church or any church for that matter, implemented to help homosexuals with their sexual/mental disorder? Zero. How many times has your church reached out to the homosexuals sitting among your very own congregation? You know who they are. They didn't enter your church to remain anonymous. They have taken over all aspects of your organizations. The homosexual interest in God is political and their ambition in your church is the steady accumulation of power. Your pastor knows this to be true; however he'd rather posture and promote theological dogma then create controversy. They'd rather keep their congregations looking towards the sky for solutions to all social ills, instead of challenging their own fear of man. Your pastors and ministers fear homosexuals more then they fear God. In the meantime, homosexuals are piling into your church like it was the steam room at the local YMCA. The weak, holy men you follow are afraid to diagnose the disease therefore they will never find a cure. By the way, YMCA stands for Young Men's Christian Association; any questions?

In June of 2008, the Canadian Governments Human Rights Commission formally ordered a Christian pastor to renounce his faith and never again express moral opposition to homosexuality. The preacher had been speaking out against homosexuality for years. He was also ordered to pay $5,000 in damages. Which begs the question to all Christians; what are you going to do when the homosexuals come for you?

The Bible and Racism/Sexism

Since the Holy Bible is the most valuable political tool ever created I think it's only fair to show you specifically who the 'Holy Bible' was expressly not written for; **Blacks**. Yeah, a lot of you will take issue with that fact but it's true. **Prove Me Wrong!** In its current form the Bible wasn't really intended for women either. The irony however, is that a majority of the parables, metaphors, prose, poetry, symbolism, fables, and stories within the book were written by ancient Africans. But the works were stolen, plagiarized, changed and corrupted and put into this one book. And it was used against the very people it was originally written for. Sure, there is ageless wisdom and good advice within the Bible, that's undeniable. There were dozens of Bibles that came before the one Christians currently use. Truth does not fear investigation; so let's begin.

From genesis to revelations the 'Holy Bibles' hatred of Blacks is strong and in your face blatant. But Black Christians for centuries have chosen to ignore that fact. It became easy for Whites to commit racist atrocities when they had religious doctrine backing them up 100% of the way. Still, Blacks around the world pour into churches whole heartedly committed to a cause they know nothing about. Most are there because their mother was there before them, and her mother before her. I guess for some that's reason enough; no further research required.

When king James gathered his cronies to ink the new testament he made sure his enemies, the Jews, were responsible for the death of God's son, Jesus; brilliant. And the world has believed that nonsense ever since. He then told us that the Bible was for both Jew and Gentile; it was not. It was originally sewn together by Jewish scholars to promote nationalism among their fragmented and enslaved peoples. It was something they could all rally behind because they had no great origins, lineage, cities, statues, pyramids, monuments, wars, leaders, kings, queens, pharaohs, or thinkers in which to claim. So the Jews proclaimed they were God's chosen people with a destiny to rule Canaan; and invented warriors and prophets like Joshua and Moses and Daniel.

But King James wanted to put his own name on this ready made religious philosophy instead of creating his own. So, he made them heroes and villains at the same time; they became God's chosen people as well as the murderers of his son. Can you blame Jewish people for not accepting the Bible? In fact, these days Israel seems to have turned more towards atheism. King James (James Stewart) and his token wife by the way were Black slave owners. They believed in the conquest and subjugation of peoples of color throughout the world. So why do people of color still cling to his book? They all say it's the message not the messenger, so let's examine exactly what this message is:

In **Genesis**, which stands for **genes of Isis**, Noah curses his young son Ham for laughing at him for staggering out of the Ark butt naked and drunk. I think that was really extreme since Noah was the one that had been knowingly drinking fermented wine. He not only curses Ham but his children, and children's children forever. Wow! Cain didn't get that harsh a treatment from God after murdering his own brother. But who were the descendants of Ham that Noah cursed? They were **Cush (Ethiopia), Mizraim, Sheba, Nimrod, Nineveh, Philistines, Amorites, Sodom, Gomorrah,** etc...All people and places that were Black. That tells us the Jews arch enemies and the giant David supposedly slew were Philistines; Black. The immoral people, whom Jonah was supposed to preach to before being swallowed up by a whale, were Black. The wicked inhabitants of Sodom and Gomorrah were Black. The Ambitious people building the tower of Babel were Black. All the Pharaohs whom the Jews despised and wanted God to destroy, were Black. In other words according to the men who wrote the Bible all the notorious villains, evil doers and people out of favor with God were Black folks.

Note the writer's jealousy in **Isaiah 18:1** *"Destruction is certain for the land of Ethiopia, which lies at the headwaters of the Nile. Its winged sailboats glide along the river, and ambassadors are sent in fast boats down the Nile. Go home, swift messengers! Take a message to your land divided by rivers, to your tall, smooth-skinned people, who are feared far and wide for their conquests and destruction...the lord will cut you off as though with pruning shears...the wild animals will gnaw at bones all winter. (New Living Translation, Tyndale House Publisher, Inc.)* He even refers to the people as "tall and smooth skinned," revealing his preoccupation with their outer appearance; jealousy. Isaiah was said to be written around 700 B.C., guess who was the Pharaoh; Piankhi or Shabaka- the 25th dynasty. Throughout the book of Isaiah, the writer rails against Philistines, Babylon, Memphis, Egypt and anywhere else heavily populated and ruled by Blacks.

It is impossible to read **Ezekiel** without getting the feeling that the writer was consumed with jealousy and hate. At one point Ezekiel claims God said 'He'd put hooks into Pharaoh's mouth and drag him like a fish.' That's just plain sick! In fact, the entire book of Ezekiel is absolutely disturbing. And **Jeremiah** isn't much different. They all seem to be consumed by their hatred of the Black nations but telling us it is God that hates these people instead of them. Throughout the Bible the underlying theme is Black is bad. In **Songs 1:5** we find a woman apologizing for being Black. Even Solomon had to defend his Blackness. *"I am Black but comely o ye women of Jerusalem."* In other words; "I may be Black but at least I'm handsome," the all wise Solomon argued in defending his color. In **Numbers 12:1** Miriam and Aaron criticized Moses for marrying a Cushite woman (a Black woman). So God cursed Miriam of course and did nothing to Aaron. But notice, God didn't address their racism but was only angry because they had the audacity to question his servant; Moses. After all **Ezra 9:2** says God doesn't want the holy race to be "polluted" by mixed marriages. That's one hell of a bold statement as well as a contradiction in facts since the Biblical Jews 'mixed' with almost every race they encountered. There is and never was a holy race. It was a lie.

Even the Ethiopian Simon pops up out of nowhere to perform manual, slave labor, by supposedly carrying the cross for Jesus. And throughout the Bible the racism goes on and on. Read it for yourself, but this time recognize its true political intent. I asked several ministers why **Leviticus 20:13** says that the penalty for homosexuality was death and if they thought God was being too hard. I also asked them why God disqualified people with physical defects from coming before him. Their only answer was that you can't question God and that everything in the Old Testament was nailed to the cross when Jesus died. But if that's the case why do they still quote the Old Testament as well as the Ten Commandments? Didn't God say "I am the same today, yesterday and always?" Did God back peddle? Or were these men simply unable to keep their lies straight? The Gospels talk about Jesus healing a dying slave because the master was about to lose a good servant. Jesus complied but instead of condemning the institution of slavery he commends the master for caring so much about his slave; unbelievable! Jesus obviously couldn't see into the future because these were the same Bible verses the slave masters would use to condone and continue their kidnapping and enslavement of Africans.

I already posed the question of why any woman would read and accept the Bible when it's full of nothing but hatred and sexism towards them. In fact, a woman would be a fool to step into a church and read from a book that says she's inferior and only capable of
producing children; specifically male children. According to the Bible a woman was the cause of mans downfall because she ate from the tree of life. But isn't a woman within herself a tree of life? We're talking about a being capable of walking around with a life growing inside of her body. Then the Creator gave her what we call milk, which includes nutrients within that same body to sustain a healthy baby. If that isn't a tree of life I don't know what is. A woman started civilization when the first man came from her birth canal. Whether you believe in creation or evolution a woman started life on this planet.

But the same jealous, egotistical men, who told us God was a 'He,' decided that as they rewrote His-Story, Her-Story would be one of servitude and ineptness. The handful of women mentioned in the Bible are there to serve and cater to men; all of them. From Eve to Ester to Mary, you can't show me one woman in the Bible who wasn't there to serve the pleasure and ego of a man. As the centuries went by men used the Bibles depiction and description of women to psychologically subdue and keep them oppressed. Whenever a woman would start thinking for herself a man would use scripture to remind her of her place in the home and in society. And if she still wouldn't shut up, they would burn her at the stake or call her a communist and now-a-days a whore.

A much needed recap

During the late 1800 European Egyptologist Samuel Birch entered (some say desecrated) the final resting place of the African Pharaoh's. As he marveled at the detailed, intricate hieroglyphs of these colorful, majestic symbols, a most startling revelation presented itself. As he detailed and deciphered the signs and symbols of this ancient civilization, he discovered the most closely guarded secret the world still refuses to believe; these Egyptians, these dark skinned pyramid builders, were the minds that gave the world its afterlife concept. That's right; rebirth, baptism, last rites, resurrection and the entire foundation that is today's Christianity was conceived by this ancient culture. It was these Africans that gave God consciousness to the world. And from there it spread as did their science and technology.

The Greek historians document their studies in Egypt. Quite naturally they took what they learned with them; as did all other cultures and languages. Everything has its precedent; everything. That goes double for today's religious rituals and trappings. For centuries, depicted on the walls of the Luxor (for this study I'm using the Greek names because they hold familiarity with the reader) in what is called Egypt, is the 4,000 year old story of **Horus** the sun god. The hieroglyph shows his mother **Isis** being visited by the 'holy goat'- a being with the body of a man and the head of a goat. He tells her she will have a baby without the sperm of a man. Her miracle child **Horus**, who is born from her virgin womb, healed the sick, performed miracles, had twelve followers, died and rose again three days later, would become the foundation for every religion known to man-kind. These were their gods. This was their belief system. Egyptian theology was the foundation for Christian monopoly.

They were just as convinced and dedicated to their theology as Christians are today; except, in many ways they were wrong. We know they were wrong because when their tombs were plundered their earthly wealth and mummified remains were still inside. They expected to take their human forms, earthly wealth and human concepts into the after life. Just like the Christians who mimic them 4,000 years later, are wrong. It is fear of the grave that causes Christians to ignore all the facts, close their eyes to simple logic, and hide reasonable explanations-just to believe. No matter what walk of life, social construct, educational level, or racial background, fanaticism knows no boundaries. Its cause has no restraints, no morality, or has any relation to God. This theology has prompted religious wars, persecution, sexism, racism, greed, and murder; all in the name of the lord.

The violent and bloody roots of Christianity are well documented by hundreds of years of bloodshed and pain. *'A bad tree can't produce good fruit'* can it? In 1492 the Pope blessed one of the first slave ships, **'Good ship Jesus'** whose coat of arms was two Africans back to back with their wrists bound. The pope called Africans "infidels" and said God had ordained slavery against the **African**; (sound familiar). **Pope Nicholas V** knew that without slavery Rome and the early Catholic Church would not have been able to carry on. Black flesh was the life's blood that flowed through the Vatican. The Catholic Church was built on the blood of slaves. In 1839 and 1866 the holy office of the Vatican sent out statements expressly condoning slavery with God's blessing. Today, when I look at all the ignorant so called **African-Americans** running around claiming to be Catholic, I just shake my head. And I'm sure the spirits of their ancestors do the same.

Religious doctrine is rarely researched but constantly quoted and conditionally obeyed. I say conditionally because no matter what religion they subscribe to, Christians, Muslims and Jews cherry pick the passages that suit them best. The authenticities of their so called holy books are never publicly debated by Evangelists or Rabbis' because it would be a colossal embarrassment. A humiliated 'holy man' cannot hold power for long. **The psychology behind organized religion was not meant to prevent you from doing things you ordinarily wouldn't do, but to create residual revenue from your doing what comes naturally.**

'Urging humans to be super humans, on pain of death and torture, is the urging of terrible self-abatement at their repeated and inevitable failure to keep the rules.'
-Christopher Hitchens

To keep people locked inside a spiritual jail only personifies their eventual escape. Once free they'll do anything to stay free and everything to forget their enslavement. They will often embrace the things religions withheld and made them believe was evil. A man/woman abruptly disconnected from their indoctrination (religion) will seek solace in 'worldly' ways. They often abuse their physical bodies to fill the void left in their spiritual bodies. That's one of the reasons why we always hear about some big time devout Christian leaving the church and running a muck; essentially doing the exact opposite of their indoctrination.

Repression leads to perversion. Forcing a priest (who's still a male) to take a vow of celibacy creates and invites perversion. The fable of Adam and Eve makes clear; God wanted every living thing to have a mate, no exceptions. The biblical story of Noah's Ark strongly reiterates opposite sex companionship by giving every man, woman and animal aboard the ark its mate. Although a myth, it shows how far back the ideology of man and woman as mates goes back. Why do people confess and take advice from a priest who doesn't have a degree in psychology, who's never been married and spends his days with little boys on his lap? Certain human behaviors don't require the church or government to sanction as right or wrong. We intuitively know right from wrong, but choose to ignore it.

When things that are normal to your development is within your view yet withheld and suppressed for too long, when finally allowed to consume it, human nature makes us gorge ourselves silly from going without for so long and fear that we may not get it again.

That especially includes sex. Once again, sexual repression leads to perversion. Take a close look at abstinence only programs. Partisan social activists and religious organizations help push this nonsense to our children. Social conservatives, as they call themselves, are opposed to safe sex as an option to make teens fully aware of their choices. As a way to skirt the rules without breaking them, oral sex has seen a dramatic increase as with mouth and throat diseases in teens. <u>One in four high school teen girls has a sexually transmitted disease.</u> A billion dollar failure, abstinence only programs do not work. Yet religious fanatics refuse to see anything other then Jesus Christ and the Bible. If priests and ministers can't remain celibate, how abstinent do you expect a 16 year old boy with raging hormones to be? And in case you wanted to know... priests taking a vow of celibacy has nothing to do with GOD. The early church had problems with wives and the children of priests looking and expecting money or property when a married priest died. So, in order to keep everything the priest owned and not end up in court, they came up with the vow of celibacy. That wasn't very complicated at all.

The number one problem in a social dictatorship is that its leaders impose ridiculous rules that are extremely difficult to obey and that they themselves are unable to adhere to; while it is the domination and rigid implementation of these rules by the privileged 'few', that keeps the 'many' blind to their own servitude.

Jimmy Swaggart/ Jim Baker/ Yahwey Ben Yawhwey/ David Koresh/   Jim Jones/ Malachi York/ Jesse Jackson (the list goes on and on)-all were accused, confessed, or convicted of being unable to keep their zippers up. Kind of makes you want to run to a woman preacher, huh.

The Pastors, Reverends and Popes who pass down judgment and guilt have never met up to the standards they demand from their followers. History past and present reveals this overwhelming fact. **Again, note the relationship between the religious hierarchy and homosexuality:**

Christian Televangelist **Paul Crouch**, founder of **Trinity Broadcasting Network** (TBN), the world's largest Christian television network, reportedly engaged in a shameless sexual relationship with a TBN employee; Enoch Lonnie Ford. Ford, a convicted child molester, received $425,000 in hush money from Crouch to keep quiet about his and Crouch's homosexual relationship. However, Ford came back demanding ten million dollars more. Ford alleges that Paul Crouch often forced him to have sexual relations in order to keep his job. The affair came to light after the two 'gay lovers' had a falling out. (Los Angeles Times, Sept.12, 2004)

Christian minister **Ted Haggard,** the leader of 30 million **Evangelicals**, loved having 'gay' sex while at the same time preaching against homosexuality. He paid a male prostitute for sex and drugs on a regular basis. He also liked having young males watch as he masturbated. *"You can be a man of God and you can have a little bit of fun on the side,"* he allegedly told one young man while he watched him stroked his penis.

Christian, Sunday school teacher, **Malissa Huckaby,** raped 8 year old **Sandra Cantu** with a foreign object, killed her, then stuffed her body inside a suitcase and threw it into a pond. I can't help but wonder how many children in her Sunday school class she fantasized about killing before actually choosing her own daughter's playmate.

The architects of organized religion are the same Christians who told everybody the world was flat and said it was heresy to believe otherwise. Were they so obtuse or stupid not to look up and see that the Sun and Moon themselves were round? What if I told you God wanted you to lick the puss filled sores of your fellow Christians? Would you do it? I bet you'd think I was crazy. But early Christians did it. In fact, they believed the more you suffered and lived in filth and pain the closer you were to God. Sound a bit familiar? Early Christians licked every puss filled wound, scab and cut of the hurt or ailing to be closer to God. Early Christians licked the white sores of lepers and refused to bathe for years at a time; especially women.

Can you imagine a woman not bathing for years because the pastor told her that her suffering smell would bring her closer to God? Saint Agnes never bathed in her life. She died at age 13, of filth I suppose; all because she and those around her believed the lies of money grubbing priests. In the Catholic Church a lot of their parishioners who achieved 'sainthood' did so by way of filth and disease. Furthermore, parishioners would give their little boys for priests to have their way with. They were told that in doing so they'd move up in the Christian ranks while gaining favor with God. Monks were well known to have sex with little boys and animals to keep from breaking their vows of celibacy. Now days, little boys are not outright given, tribute is implied by parental remittance of alter boys.

A myth is an idea that is widely believed but is actually false. A religious myth controls thinking and thereby action or inaction. Those who question the religious myth are identified as evil, irreverent or sacrilegious. The religious hierarchy will not engage in public debate with them because their facts will put an end to the myth. The European hypocrisy wants their lies and legacy of lies to last forever. But can we still afford to let lies flourish as truth? Who are the beneficiaries of these lies and why do we fear them? Have they become our Gods? Our future depends on what we learn from the past. What do we owe our children if not the truth?

Turning a Blind Eye

Why are people so unable or unwilling to distinguish between righteousness and ***those*** *evil men who use religion to disguise their real aims? The unthinking* **Muslim or Christian would likely believe that his/*her* religion is being attacked rather then those conquerors** *and enslavers and pedophiles and con men and opportunists* **who disgraced it in covering their desire for wealth and world domination.**
 - Chancellor Williams, historian (Italics mine)

I've got a few questions for you to think about. If you knew the little boy who lived next door to you was being molested, what would you do? Would you call the police? Would you at least alert Child Protective Services? Or would you think it was none of your business and do absolutely nothing? What if it were your child? The one thing you wouldn't do is protect the child molester, would you? These are the questions Pope Benedict XVI should have been asking himself. And now these are the questions you have to ask yourself about Pope Benedict XVI and the entire Catholic hierarchy. When I heard that a priest had molested over 200 little deaf boys I shook my head. When the New York Times reported that Pope Benedict XVI himself covered up the crimes I cringed. You see, it's a known fact that pedophiles protect other pedophiles. In 1962 the Catholic Church galvanized the already centuries old practice of baring priests from turning other priests over to the authorities. Not only do they feel that they are above the law but that the bodies of the children left in their care aren't worth protecting.

Can you imagine being an 8 year old deaf boy, who's already being ignored and shunned by the rest of the world, trying to explain to an adult that your mentor and priest keeps pulling down your pants? Does the child reconcile this betrayal in his young mind by thinking he's helping God? Does the priest tell the boy that he's doing God's work? Who knows? But one thing is for certain; no one was there who gave a dam- then or now. The crime was repulsive. The cover up was horrible. But do you still believe that these disgusting human beings ever represented God? In March of 2010, the Pope called the allegations "petty gossip." But if you were to interview the 200 boys that father Lawrence Murphy molested, I bet you'd find that some have committed suicide, some are male prostitutes, and some think that they themselves are homosexual. I guarantee that most of them have struggled in relationships their entire lives; angry, full of distrust, in and out of jail. And quite a few I'm sure went on to molest hundreds of boys themselves. Petty gossip, I think not. I've seen numerous cases were a mother was charged for being an accessory to the abuses her husband committed against their children, while she watched and did nothing.

So how are Popes, cardinals, priests, bishops or evangelists above the law when it comes to raping other people's children? These crimes against humanity have been going on within the Catholic Church since its conception. The hierarchy of this non-profit money machine has no ethics, morality, conscience or obligation except aiding and abetting fellow child molesters. But here's a frequently overlooked fact; homosexual priests can't prey on children if the children's parents don't let them. What does that mean? Any Catholic who allowed their son to be an alter boy knew the risks but ignored them. They put religion over the safety of their own children. Shame on them! Shame on them all!

Buried Beneath Jesus

I once asked a devout Christian why he said "Amen" at the end of his prayers. He told me that it was taught to him as a child by the pastor of his mother's church. So, I asked the pastor of his mother's church the same question. He told me that "Amen" meant it's finished, or I'm done. I then asked him if he'd ever heard of Ahmenhotep? He said "no," and I immediately realized a majority of the Christians in America had a lot of information withheld from them; but most notably the Black Christians. And here's why:

The indigenous brown and dark skin peoples living in what we now call America were in fact not Christians before the arrival of Christopher Columbus. Why is it that after Columbus' arrival the God they served was no longer good enough? It is a fact that the lying, rapist, pedophile Christopher Columbus forced Christianity upon the native populations. Blacks in America today are Christians because of Columbus, which still brings into question the validity of their religion and the source of their conversion. Today, Black people saying that they are Christians are in fact saying that Columbus was right and their own ancestors were wrong. Columbus will tell you as much. Go and read his captains log for yourself.

Black Americans do not research but instead accept the word of a gang of mercenaries who until the 1490's thought the world was flat. A vast number of Black folks will say "listen to the message and not the messenger." Well guess who sent Columbus? The Pope; physically the Queen of Spain but psychologically the church blessed his murder and enslavement of the Black (native) populations. Of course some of you will take issue with the **fact** that I called the natives that were living here "Black people." **Fact** is; one of the biggest myths in American history is that all Black people came here on slave ships from Africa. That is a lie. A vast majority of the Black people in America today are the descendants of the people Columbus found when he arrived hundreds of years ago. Sure millions of Blacks were kidnapped from Africa and bought here to work but there were millions already here when Columbus arrived. The tribes he never saw, captured or enslaved lived on, and today so do their children.

Natives who refused to live on reservations or left the reservation were always classified as "Negro" to prevent them or their children from someday claiming land and title. Was Columbus right? It is utter stupidity to serve a god and accept the words of people who hated and enslaved you. Since every Christian who came after Columbus believed and acted as he did (slavery and segregation) Christianity should feel like a curse word coming out of the mouth of every Black person in America. If the God your ancestors served wasn't good enough before Columbus beat them over the head with the cross, tortured, threatened and coerced them into accepting Jesus Christ and Christianity, then what is? While some of you are just figuring out Columbus didn't discover America or anything else for that matter, the rest of us already know that anything he said out of his mouth was also a lie. Columbus' real legacy is slavery, disease and religion. And one would have to be a self hating, self debasing fool to want any of the three. To bow down to Columbus' religion not only brings shame upon your ancestors but keeps future generations his slaves forever.

The Conspirators-
and Their Plans for the World

A Simple Plan

About twenty years ago two homosexual males put into words what many homosexuals had been brainstorming for years; **how do we make the world love us and be more like us?** This groundbreaking book was a milestone in what was called the "gay rights movement." *'After the Ball: How America will conquer its Fear and Hatred of Gay in the 90's'*, was a homosexual, cultural breakthrough. Countless homosexuals read the book and set out to achieve its goals. The authors, Hunter Madsen, a social scientist, and Marshall Kirk, a researcher in neuropsychiatry, planned to attack the average everyday Joe's mind and heart through a relentless and on-going mis-information campaign. They told all homosexuals to use every form of media to portray 'gays' in a positive light and to hide, filter or bury any news that exposed homosexuals in a negative way.

They designed a public relations strategy that involved the following:

Desentisitization- Flooding straight Americans with marketing and advertising that presented homosexuals in the least offensive manner.

Jamming- Equate the fear of homosexuals with the hatred of Blacks, Jews and Women.

Conversion- Present images of homosexuals as normal.

It also contained eight strategic principles for public attention:

1. Don't just express yourself, communicate
2. Appeal to the ambivalent skeptics
3. Keep talking about 'gayness'
4. Keep your issue focused: the issue is homosexuality
5. Portray 'gays' as victims, not as aggressive challengers
6. Give potential protectors a just cause
7. Make homosexuals look good
8. Make victimizers look bad

Kirk and Madsen said 'gays must be portrayed as victims in need of protection so that straights will be inclined by reflex to adopt the role of protector....straight people will not defend homosexuality, most would rather attach their protective impulse to some law.' They also advise the use of 'propagandistic advertising to depict all opponents of the 'gay' movement as homophobic, hate filled bigots. They contend that people are stupid enough to believe the allegations 'without facts, logic or proof ....and a persons beliefs can be altered whether he is conscious of the attack or not.'

Homosexuals were telling the world they're plans to attack the minds of 'straights' decades ago. Homophobic, although a made up word, gave the world a symptom to which there was no disease. They told us it was a fear of homosexuals that raised the criticism. In actuality, it was dislike, distaste, distain, disapproval and any other kind of 'dis' that led to the condemnation.

To the surprise of many, the book also contained what the author's refer to as 'gay misbehavior.' They meticulously list areas of concern while expressing blunt honesty about the lifestyle and homosexuality in general. The following are the observations and admissions of homosexuals themselves:

Gays suffer from narcissistic personality disorder. They are pathological, self absorbed with a need for constant attention and admiration, a lack of empathy or concern for others, quickly bored, shallow, interested in fads, seductive, overemphasis on appearance, superficially charming, promiscuous, exploitative, preoccupied with remaining youthful, relationships alternate between over idealization and devaluation....relationships between gay men don't usually last long. They quickly tire of their partners and fall victim to temptation. The cheating ratio of married, gay males, given enough time, approaches 100%.

A high percentage of 'gays' are pathological liars and con men....gays tend to reject all forms of morality and value judgments....a very sizable population of gay males who have been diagnosed HIV positive and continue to have unprotected sex display narcissism....gays indulge in sex in public bathrooms and think it antigay harassment when it is stopped. Many think they have the right to pursue or harass straight males, including children.

The majority of gays are extremely promiscuous and self indulgent....many are single minded sexual predators fixated on youth and physical beauty alone. When it comes to the old or ugly gays, they are the real queer bashers. Disillusioned, they are cynical about love....even friendships are based on the sexual test and are hard to sustain. Unattractive gay men find it nearly impossible to find a friend, let alone a lover....gays tend to deny reality in various ways; wishful thinking, paranoia, illogic, emotionalism and embracing crackpot ideas.

Keep in mind this is the diagnosis of two homosexual, Ivy League educated, intellectual researchers. Is there any question that anyone who exhibits the above traits is in desperate need of help? Maybe Kirk and Madsen were trying to warn the world about what was to come. Maybe this was their atonement for violating the natural laws of the universe. I don't know, but chapter six of a book written by homosexuals about furthering homosexuality, revealed far more then the world could have ever imagined.

The 'Gay Marriage' Memo

In 2008 nine of the largest homosexual activist organizations issued a joint statement advising couples against lawsuits in their home states or in federal court. Why? Because losses in those lawsuits could set the 'gay marriage' movement back for years. The memo, entitled "Make Change, Not Lawsuits" was signed by Lambda Legal, the American Civil Liberties Union, Human Rights Campaign, and the Gay and Lesbian Advocates and Defenders (GLAD), among others.

These groups have secretly worked together for years, fearing public knowledge would create a backlash. This pubic statement is the first time they revealed a unilateral hand, boldly operating together to promote "gay marriage" and "gay rights." The document laments that:

"The fastest way to win the freedom to marry throughout America is by getting marriage through state courts (to show that fairness requires it) and state legislature (to show that people support it)." It goes on to say: "We need to start with states where we have the best odds of winning. When we've won a critical mass of states, we can then turn to Congress and the federal courts. At that point, we'll ask that the U.S. government treat all marriages equally. And we'll ask that all states give equal treatment to all marriages and civil unions that are celebrated in other states..."

"...But one thing couples shouldn't do is sue the federal government or, if they are from other states, go sue their home state or their employer to recognize their marriage or open up the health plan. Pushing the federal government before we have a critical mass of states recognizing same-sex relationships or suing in states where the courts aren't ready is likely to get us bad rulings. Bad rulings will make it much more difficult for us to win marriage, and will certainly make it take much longer..."

"...As society gets more used to gay and lesbian couples being married, it will be easier to win cases in states that look iffy now. In a few years, the cases just won't seem like such a big jump. If we plunge ahead and lose cases in those states now, the courts will have to overrule themselves later to go our way. That usually takes a few years at least, and often much longer. That means it is likely to take longer to get a good decision than it would have taken if we hadn't brought a case early on and lost it..."

"The history is pretty clear: the U.S. Supreme Court typically does not get too far ahead of either public opinion or the law in the majority of states…That makes the California campaign of prime importance…marriage in California will transform the national debate on the freedom to marry. It will do that because the decision is well-reasoned constitutional law from the most influential state court in the nation…"

Media Control and Bias

'The Vagina Monologues' originally included the sexual assault of a thirteen year old girl by a twenty-four year old woman who got the little girl drunk and proceeded to have her way with her. As a result of this rape, the thirteen year old minor, converts to lesbianism and thanks the twenty-four year old rapist for converting her. This is significant for several reasons; first, it demonstrates how the mind of its homosexual writer works and judging from the accolades bestowed upon the writer by other homosexuals, one could argue they all share the same mindset and goals. Second, it gives predatory ideas to a fringe group of homosexuals that will in fact go out and try to enact what they've seen. But wasn't that the writer's intent; to plant seeds of perversion, water them, and not take any responsibility for their growth? Third, it wasn't until straight, as opposed to crooked, heterosexuals objected that the scene was removed.

Interestingly enough, since a lot of authors interject auto-biographical scenes into their work, one can only guess if the author has engaged in such desperate, despicable, predatory and illegal actions herself. On pages 103-104 of the 10th anniversary edition of *The Vagina Monologues* author Eve Ensler asks an unnamed 6 year old girl the following questions:

1 If your vagina got dressed what would it wear?
2 If it could speak what would it say?
3 What does your vagina remind you of?
4 What's special about your vagina?
5 What does your vagina smell like?

As weird and sick as they are, remember, these questions were aimed at a six year old child. This is as glaring an example of predatory behavior as I've ever seen.

That brings me to this carefully hidden bit of information. **"Hundreds of lesbian gangs across the nation are attacking and raping young girls in schools and other public locations."**- The Eyewitness News Everywhere, 6/30/07. The article reads: Gangs known as GTO's or "Gays taking over," are attacking school girls….a deputy in the

Shelby county gang unit said 'lesbian gang members will sodomize[with sex toys] and are forcing young girls to perform all sexual acts. They are forcing themselves on our children....they carry weapons and will use them quicker than any male.' The report also included a list of Memphis schools where such incidents were documented. The gay activist group GLAAD threatened to sue the Memphis TV station in an attempt to block the lesbian gang report. But the report went out anyway and hopefully some girls were able to protect or defend themselves against these homosexual attacks. Once again, homosexuals were more concerned with their image then in the safety of our children.

A video containing actual classroom footage of teachers imposing pro-homosexual propaganda on children, as young as six, has been circulating. The video follows a Massachusetts schools fourth annual gay and lesbian pride day activities. The video also contains clips from the 1996 homosexual film "It's Elementary."

ABC NEWS ONLINE- Dutch shock over HIV rape gang:

A gang of homosexuals drugged, raped and infected with HIV men they lured over the internet. Police arrested three seropositive homosexual men after four victim's ages 25-50 accused them of rape and premeditated bodily harm. The police chief in the northern town of Groningen said two of the four men had confessed. Their motive: 'It excited them, and the more HIV infected people there were the better their chances of unprotected sex. They considered unprotected sex to be pure'. According to police and prosecutors, eight more victims have come forward since the case was publicized. Some of the men were not only raped but injected with contaminated blood.

In Germany-and working its way here to America....A subsidiary of the **Ministry for Family Affairs** encourages parents to **sexually message their children as young as 1-3 years of age.** Two forty page booklets entitled **'Love, Body and Playing Doctor'** are distributed by the **German Federal Health Education Center. For ages 4-6 the booklet recommends teaching children the movements of copulation.** Millions of copies of this book are distributed yearly. Regardless of their reasons for recommending the molestation of their children, Germany has become a pedophiles paradise.

Meanwhile....In the homosexual Castro district of San Francisco, homosexuals assaulted a small group of Christian missionaries who had to be escorted out of the area by over a dozen armed police officers. If you want to see a mob of **'gays gone wild'** go to "**YouTube; Chased Out Of The Castro District.**" It's pretty disturbing. **Note: no one was arrested in these assaults.**

What you don't know can hurt you!

Just like you, I wanted to know why the public wasn't getting this urgent information concerning the unprovoked attacks by homosexuals. We know that the government carefully screens, manipulates and filters its information. But for quite some time now media outlets have been influenced and controlled by agenda based homosexuals who don't give a damn about public safety, family, our children or anything that doesn't fit their 'program'.

After years of pressure from homosexual lobbyists **The AP (Associated Press)** now tells its writers to *"avoid references to 'sexual preference' or to gay or alternative lifestyle."* The **New York Times** tells its writers to avoid the term *"admitted homosexual"* because that *"suggests criminality or shame."* They are also told to avoid the term *"gay rights"* because *"advocates for gay issues are concerned that the term may invite resentment by implying 'special rights' that are denied other citizens."* Instead, the phrase *"equal rights"* or *"civil rights"* should be used. Also **New York Times** writers must never use *'sexual preference'*, because it *"carries the disputed implication that sexuality is a matter of choice."* There are thousands of news outlets around the country that people depend upon to give them facts. If sexual orientation has anything to do with a news story the public has a right to know.

In Related News….

Almost every newspaper in California promotes same- sex marriage by publishing same-sex wedding announcements. Slowly but surely a battle weary public is changing their attitudes about seeing these notices and eventually gay activists hope they'll be agreeing to these unions. GLAAD reported that well over a thousand daily U.S. newspapers accept wedding announcements from gay and lesbian couples. The homosexual friendly New York Times has since opened their weddings/celebrations section allowing homosexual couples to make their announcements. GLAAD launched this campaign to promote same sex wedding announcements to make the public use to seeing them. This is a strategy to inch more and more into the public's psychological acceptance of same-sex couples and eventually legislation. It's always political, always. This tactic is used to invoke an emotional response of sympathy from readers who remember their own time of celebration. This attempt to bring similarities of normalcy between the homosexual lifestyle and the heterosexual lifestyle is shrewd and will result in nothing less then the obliteration of the family.

Media bias keeps any negative images of homosexuals closely guarded. But once in a while, by mistake or sheer boldness, someone will decide to expose the public to the truth. <u>**Queer As Folk**</u> was a television program that should have been on pay- per- view.

The one dimensional, testosterone driven plots were always about homosexual males obsessed with sex. This cable program showed in graphic detail homosexual males having anal sex, oral sex, group sex, phone sex, sex with minors, assault and battery sex (sadomasochism), and sex for money. Despite the explicit scenes the show received highly favorable reviews from big time media outlets. Why, because most media outlets have been hijacked by homosexuals and/or subscribe to the homosexual agenda. Producer Tony Jonas told the *New York Times* **"we don't have to apologize for or whitewash or pretend what gay sexuality is all about."** *It's all about sex and a sex-style.* Indeed, he was 'keeping it real'. But it's also about perverting as many people as possible. *(Please see Webster's definition of perversion).* Well then, if gay sexuality is all about sex, why the big sham about gay marriage and adopting children?

...And the media blitz continues on what we call plain or regular TV (television without cable), I was watching an episode of **Judge Mathis** and the entire half hour was about homosexual sex and how much fun they had. I know these judge shows are for entertainment purposes, but I thought I was watching an episode of Jerry Springer. Then there was the alleged 'gay' **Judge David Young** whose promo stated he 'gives justice with a snap'; a known homosexual phrase; more indoctrination.

It's not much of a stretch from a homosexual judge to a 'pro gay' talk show host who wears more make-up then Tammy Faye Bakker. If you've ever watched the **Tyra Bank's Show**, it's apparent that she is paid by homosexuals to promote homosexuality. On a regular basis she applauds homosexuality and 'begs' viewers to 'come out of the closet'. Her day-time talk show is yet another medium by which to sway 'straight' America into submission and acceptance.

On her other show, the culture corrupting **America's Next Top Model,** homosexual males are strategically placed in front of and behind the scenes. Here, the European definition of style and beauty is personified and applauded, while young girls trade in their innocence for vanity and superficiality. This show, controlled by people who have nothing to offer society but ridiculous caricatures and exploitation, allows homosexual males the rare opportunity to publicly feast off the dreams and vulnerability of young women; in order to fill the empty void left by their own confused sexuality. Consumed by their misconceived ideas of beauty, these gay males ridicule and mock women in order to give credibility to their own miserable existence. The shows ability to manipulate and bring out the worst in our children is without shame.

The judges, who lack even the superficial beauty required of their own contestants, are given the power to say who stays and who goes. In the guise of constructive criticism, homosexual males who wish they were women, bash and critique qualities in women that they can only dream of possessing. With sometimes visceral contempt, they tear down the same traits, gestures and mannerisms they themselves are always emulating. The oddity they refer to as **Miss J**, has the audacity to be teaching females how to walk, stand and posture like a woman should. Somehow he's convinced himself that he is something other than a male. In every category there's a male teaching a female how to be a woman. In what parallel universe can that possibly be correct? What a farce. A lawyer can't teach a med student how to be a doctor. It's disturbing. For years **America's Next Top Model** has allowed male homosexuals to take their jealous frustrations out on these young, inexperienced girls while Americans sit back and enjoy the spectacle. By allowing homosexuals to adjudicate and bash naïve, young women and their aspirations, we essentially sit back and watch as they become the judges over us all; telling us what's beautiful, what's important, what's moral and most importantly, what's normal. God help us all!

Then there's **Ellen Degeneres** who turned out to be a homosexual, propaganda bonanza. With exceptional wit and charm, she was able to convince some of the most starch heterosexuals that being gay was 'fun and fantastic'. Once she garnered the support of her studio audience, ratings skyrocketed. From day one, her show played a pivotal role in painstakingly crafting the new, gracious, pleasant picture of the female homosexual. The 'butch-dyke' of yesterday was causing too much drama. Her image was a stark contrast from the rude, obnoxious **Rosie O'Donnel** who told us that standing on her head helped her depression. Ellen has consistently promoted, protected and redefined the public image of the female homosexual. For several years now, almost every sitcom or drama has a homosexual character among its cast or written into the script. You can't even get a commercial made today without a homosexual on stand-by.

I remember watching **Dave Chappelle** on **Oprah** talking about his refusal to wear a dress in a movie. He said that there had to be some kind of conspiracy to make Black actors wear a dress a some point in their career. Since Hollywood began I've always seen White male actors put on lipstick, wigs, high heels and dresses. From Bugs Bunny to The Kids in the Hall, gender bending was their norm. But mainstream Black actors had for so long refused; (and I'm not talking about **Flip Wilson's** comedy routines). I began seeing a disturbing pattern emerge; the hard-core tough guy, Black males began wearing dresses; something you never would have seen in the 1970's. And the more these males put on dresses and acted feminine the 'gate keepers' made them even bigger stars. They got more roles, bigger budgets and whopping paychecks. Wesley snipes, **Ving Rhames** and **Eddie Murphy** went from tough guys to cross dressing, switch hitters overnight. **Martin Lawrence** and **Will Smith** both put on dresses, compromised their integrity and sent these images out around the world.

And every time we sit back and say nothing the more these images are forced upon us. The homosexual ogre in the new **'Shrek Forever After'** is further proof of that. It also reiterates my wider point that homosexuals will go to any lengths to get into the minds of our children. Why was it necessary to put a homosexual character in an animated children's movie? The intention is to push the envelope and if nobody says or does anything, in a few years they'll make an entire children's movie starring a homosexual character. When is enough, enough?

The powerful, homosexual, Hollywood elite constantly transmit their agenda into every home in America unabated. Even before weirdo **Dennis Rodman** put on that wedding gown, the indescribable **Marilyn Manson** and tough guy **Arnold Schwarzenegger** ('Junior') had already prepared Americans for uni-sexuality on screen. By the time **Thomas Beatie** got his pregnant stomach rubbed on Oprah it wasn't all that shocking to hear *"pregnant man has baby boy!"* Rest assured this 'new man' who won't be classified as male or female, will be forced upon us. They (the homosexual elite) intend to create these genetically altered unisexual 'people' and their first step is to use the mass media to prepare society for this **New World Order.**

The Homosexual Factory

If I told you that there were brick buildings throughout America were a heterosexual man could walk inside and when he came out he'd be homosexual, I bet you wouldn't believe me. In fact, you'd think I was crazy. But it's true. There are hundreds of these structures scattered throughout America. The most common name for these buildings are prisons. That's right, American penitentiaries are homosexual factories that turn out homosexual males like an assembly line at Ford.

The Romans built the first jails because they had criminals; criminals the dysfunction of their society had created. To them there was no other means of discipline then to physically trap the body and bombard the spirit with hate. Those iron bars are cages that can turn the most honorable humans into beasts. To indiscriminately cage people like animals is troublesome, costly, ineffective and created more homosexuals then the Catholic Church. It's terrifying for regular men, but when you sentence a homosexual to prison you're sending him/her into the most conducive environment imaginable. For example, when a homosexual male gets to be locked up 24 hours, 7 days a week with straight males who are in their sexual prime, he's literally in an emotional paradise. Homosexuals, being bold and aggressive as they are, will stop at nothing to violate a new heterosexual inmate.

Although some of these interactions are consensual, many are not. Voluntary homosexual activity among males who were thought to be straight and bare no signs of homosexual inclinations before incarceration have recently been classified. Modern day sociologists have given a name to consensual sex between males in prison; they call it **situational homosexuality**. This theory claims that because of their confinement males will have sex with other males because there are no women around. Yet if the only clear definition of consensual sex (according to prison officials) is someone without a knife to their throat, a lot of this data is faulty. What about instances where violence is merely implied?

Many inmates engage in what appears to be consensual sex but they are pushed by other types of coercion or violence. That does not constitute the statistics that make up situational homosexuality. The Struckman-Johnson study found that 1 in 5 inmates experienced some form of pressured or coerced sexual conduct while in prison. Often Correction officers can't distinguish between consensual sex, coercion and rape, therefore any real or comprehensive statistical analysis is unsubstantiated. Male rape victims in prison are viewed with negativity and scorn both inside and outside the walls; therefore such a crime is grossly under-reported.

In prison and now in 'homo-thug' culture, males believe that only the person who is penetrated during sex is homosexual. The fact that some males choose to be penetrated while others choose to only penetrate, reinforces the overstated fact that it (homosexuality) is exactly that; a choice. If the 'homo-thug' shares in the orgasm and helps the other male fulfill his fantasy; that's 'gay' dude. If I drive the getaway car during a robbery and share the money, am I not a bank robber too?

Believe it or not violence is used to ensure that there's no emotional attachment, that's why most male homosexuals don't consider themselves homosexual. They rationalize the rape to be more about violence then pleasure. They use their penis as a weapon to gain physical, emotional and psychological power over their victims.

"It's a way to shame a male with something he must live with for the rest of his life. To brand a man with shame is worse than killing him outright, because it destroys his identity and self-esteem as a man...prison rape leaves a man with two options; retaliate or submit. if he retaliates he will probably be injured, maybe killed. If he submits, he gives his manhood over to the aggressor." - Eran Reya

Inside, the rapist feels a perverted satisfaction. Moreover these males who rape other inmates have usually at some point been raped themselves. Prisoners who attempt suicide in prison have frequently been victims of unreported sexual assaults. Because there are few reported incidents, there is little counseling or psychiatric evaluation. This continuous raping and the accompanying feelings of powerlessness and shame has a direct link to the psychological rationalizations of perversion. The combination of a mental and physical breakdown at some point will lead the rape victim to begin the process of making his rapist happy in order to minimize the physical violence and ensure protection. Eventually the victim will begin to derive pleasure from these sexual acts and view them as a sort of duty to please the stronger males that surround him.

Anyone with common sense knows that a man serving 2-5 years shouldn't be locked up next to a man serving 25-life, no more then homosexuals shouldn't be next to 'straight' men in prison; as if sending inmates to prisons hundreds of miles away from their families, making visitation all but impossible wasn't bad enough. But it's done with the express purpose of corrupting and permanently damaging that male before releasing him back into society; emasculated and/or effeminized, psychologically damaged, emotionally detached, animalistic, and simply unable to fit back into his community. Prison officials should be charged with reckless endangerment for creating and facilitating an environment of perversion and a cycle of preventable violence.

A young White man gets thrown into prison and is raped and ordered to serve the pleasure of a group of <u>Aryan</u> skinheads. He'll bring that trauma with him when he's released from the penitentiary. A young Black man gets thrown into prison and is raped and ordered to serve the pleasure of a group of Black males who say they're not homosexual yet regularly engage in sex acts with the young male. The young Black male won't tell his family or girlfriend his closely guarded secret. In fact, upon his release he may trick his mind into believing it never happened. In both cases and between both races neither is tested for H.I.V. Today, they may be out trolling your neighborhood in search of someone weaker then them in an attempt to get their 'manhood' back. Or they could be the male prostitute you find on any street in America.

If you think that just because you're in a cage you must behave like an animal, you're wrong. If I told you that with one collect call you could save your mother, sister, or girlfriend's life, right there from your prison cell; would you do it? Would you make that one telephone call? Well, a woman you know is in grave danger from your cellmate. That's right; the man in the cell next to you gave up his manhood shortly after he arrived in prison. Every night other inmates pass him around like a cigarette. Yet every Saturday his wife and kids come to visit him. He kisses his wife's lips probably with the stink of another man's testicles still on his breath. His wife has no idea he gave up his manhood a long time ago. But you do. You know he's no longer anal-retentive, and it turns your stomach to see him in that visiting area hugged up with that loyal, devoted woman, pretending like he's done nothing wrong. As soon as he's released, he's going straight back to that woman and infect her with A.I.D.S. That's right; he's planning to kill her!

Doesn't she have a right to decide whether she wants to die or not?
He's certainly not going to tell her he's been having sex with males in prison. With an anonymous telephone call, letter or e-mail you can save a woman's life.
Before any woman pulls back the sheets to have welcome home sex with her newly released boyfriend or husband (city jail or penitentiary), she should first make him submit to an A.I.D.S test. Take him to your personal health provider or even the free clinic, let the doctor swab his mouth and wait for the results. If he loves you and has nothing to hide, he won't complain. But if he fights you tooth and nail then he could be trying to kill you; run!

 The most alarming and shameful conversation I had with a formerly incarcerated female was her disclosure of how the butch-dyke behaves in prison. *"Bull daggers in prison are five times more aggressive and violent then any male homosexual I've ever seen. I feel sorry for any woman who is sent to prison these days because she'll literally be in hell!"*
Out of control behavior in an uncontrolled environment makes the butch-dyke feel like a god. I also feel sorry for any young women being thrown into the penal system to be pounced upon by these sick inmates. God help them!

Homosexual Males Who Want To Get HIV

Wikapedia: **Bugchasing (or bug chasing)** is a slang term for a subculture of gay men who desire and actively pursue HIV
Infection. Bugchasers "chase the bug" by seeking sexual partners who are HIV positive for the purpose of having unprotected sex. **Gift givers** are HIV positive men who attempt to infect bug chasers with HIV.

Bugchasers and gift givers interact in mutually negotiated deals to help the bug chaser become HIV positive. Some bug chasers organize and participate in "bug parties" or "conversion parties," sex parties where HIV positive and negative men engage in unprotected sex, in hopes of acquiring HIV ("getting the gift.")

"In private sex clubs across the U.S. men gather to participate in what is called Russian roulette. Ten men are invited. Nine are HIV negative, one is HIV positive. The men have agreed not to speak of A.I.D.S. or HIV. They participate in as many unsafe sexual encounters with each other as possible, thus increasing their chances to receive "the bug." These are the men known as bug chasers." –Daniel Hill, Alternatives magazine issue 15

Health officials are concerned about homosexuals trolling the internet to find orgies with HIV infected males. This behavior has become a problem in the spread of HIV infection. Some bug chasers say sexual Russian roulette gives them a rush. Others want HIV because they're tired of being afraid of catching it. It would decrease their anxiety if they tested positive. They simply want to get it over with. Others want the sympathy and attention that comes with testing HIV Positive.

Bug chasers believe that by taking the drug cocktails HIV offers no chance of them dying and that in fact A.I.D.S. is practically cured. Wrong. A.I.D.S. affects everyone's body differently and some people's bodies do not respond at all to the drugs. Not to mention strains and mutations. Once again the misinformation within this sub-culture acts as a vacuum.

And just when you thought it couldn't get any worse, the perversion just keeps on coming. Few things about homosexuality surprise me; this is one of them. Can you imagine how deeply psychologically damaged an individual would have to be to purposely intend to get H.I.V.? And what does it say about the individual who is more then willing to infect him? What else is he willing to do? What other despicable acts has he committed or will he soon enact against society at large? History has already shown us.

Extremely dysfunctional people, who never learned to construct or cultivate nurturing social or intimate heterosexual relationships, will do anything to fit in where ever they can. "Bug chasing" is yet another cry for help by homosexuals. People who do not love themselves or have any real self worth always seek to push the boundaries of normalcy in an attempt to fill the empty void in their lives. Others simply want to die and take somebody with them; too afraid to buy a gun and pull the trigger, they've now found less conventional means.

Remember, many males and females turned homosexual in order to feel special; as if they finally belong. But after the novelty wears off and the realization that the spiritual connection they seek can never be found in their homosexual acts, this 'bug chasing' desperation can take hold. The Centers for Disease Control still reports high rates of infection among homosexuals and so-called bi-sexual males. They are still having unprotected sex with multiple partners some of which are females.

Famous Homosexuals in History

I've always wondered why the 'Famous Homosexuals in History' lists only included the persons homosexuals deemed worthy. If the only criteria needed was to be famous, infamous and homosexual, then why the snide attitude or bias against other homosexuals? One could argue that the people who aren't listed are not in favor with the image the homosexual hierarchy wants to project? They immediately got thrown under the homosexual bus as soon as their 'dark sides' were exposed. The object of these lists is to portray homosexuals as kind, sensitive, loving, creative people who wouldn't hurt a fly. And some of them are, but sadly most of them are not. After reading my list of <u>famous homosexuals in history</u> you'll see why:

Michael Swango- estimated to have poisoned to death between 30 – 60 people.
Wayne Williams-called the Atlanta Child Murderer, linked to 12 of the 30 young Black boys found murdered.
Jeffrey Dahmer-you can't say the words serial killer without mentioning Dahmer. He confessed to murdering 17 fellow homosexual males; saving, storing and eating their body parts.
Luis Alfredo Gavarito-tied, tortured, raped and murdered at least 200 children (some say more). He revealed the whereabouts of 114 bodies; ages 8-13.
Aileen Wournos-executed in 2002. Convicted of murdering seven "johns"
Charles Manson-wanted to start a 'race war' between Blacks and Whites. He sent his henchmen on a murder spree to make everyone think that members of the Black Panther Party were the killers. Manson was convicted of murdering six people.
John Wayne Gacy-loved forcing himself on little boys. He often dressed up like a circus clown to fool children into trusting him. He sadistically murdered 33 boys and buried them under his house. (Sounds kind of like Benjamin Franklin)
William Bonin-Child molester and murderer convicted of 10 murders but admitted to killing 21 fellow homosexual males.

*Note: *Almost half the mass murderers (serial killers) in U.S. history were homosexual or so called bi-sexual. And the vast majority of their victims practiced homosexuality. As it turns out homosexuals have more to fear from other homosexuals then from heterosexual hate crimes.* ***The 8 famous homosexuals listed above have murdered over 350 people between them!***

Andrew Cunanan-Killed five fellow homosexual males. Known best for the murder of fashion designer Gianni Versace.

Dean Corll-committed 28 known murders of boys ages 13-18 years old. Corll shot and strangled, pulled out pubic hair, inserted objects up their rectums, chewed off their genitals, and inserted glass rods into the shaft of their penis'. He even castrated many victims while they were still alive and sealed the severed genitals in plastic bags.

King James-Born James Stewart, best known for his 'Holy Bible' killed most of his male lovers when he was done with them. He also killed his mother.

Constintine- Emperer, best known for torturing and forcing Christianity upon millions and making Christianity a mandatory religion, persecuted and executed tens of thousands of people. He had sex with his sisters and killed many of his own family members which also included his mother. All in the name of Jesus of course.

Rev. James Cleveland-Allegedly infected young males with H.I.V. before dying of A.I.D.S. himself.

Christopher Columbus-Mass murderer, rapist and kidnapper; best known for starting the transatlantic slave trade.

Marquis De Sade-invented torturous sex. Enjoyed inserting objects up victims anus' as well as his own. He committed the most depraved sex acts the world has ever known. The term "sadism" was derived from his name.

Lizzie Borden- Allegedly killed her mother and father with an ax.

Adolf Hitler-enough said.

*Note: Most of the homosexuals listed above were all devout Christians.

Analysis and Solution

Modify thoughts/change behavior

"So as a man thinketh so he is." Or something like that. Who's telling you what to think? Power, casual sex and pornography rule the day. When did the children of the 'ME' generation move in next door? Women are constantly being told to use the people around them as **'accessories'** ; when they get tired of using or wearing them replace them or put them back on the shelf. A lot of women who are insecure, scared and have been hurt, are the first to advise others to use and abuse the next person. In doing so they'll have the upper hand and the power not to be hurt again.

"Men should be treated like accessories." I've heard White women spew that nonsense for years. It is that exact kind of thinking that has the world so screwed up right now. No one likes to be used. People are not accessories to be worn or played with. They are living, breathing, and walking complications and contradictions who just want to be loved and understood. If this negative thinking keeps up we'll all wake up one morning to find ourselves pawns in each other's deceptive games.

Casual sex and pornography, subtle and overt, rule the day. The way men and women view each other has drastically changed. Therefore, the way men and women treat each other has drastically changed. You can't have one without the other; women are sex objects and men are interchangeable tools. There is no intimacy; just sex. There is no love; just sex. Sex is the new stimulant for depression, boredom, popularity and maintaining friendships. Since homosexuality is sex without responsibility this new, tragic social condition is a win, win for all homosexuals. In the meantime divorce continues to skyrocket, single parent homes are the norm, and abortion is just a mere inconvenience that makes you miss a day off work. God, how did we get so screwed up?

Genealogy Lost Forever

The unfortunate circumstance of the single mother having her only son become homosexual is an unbearable heartbreak. The hurt, frustration and anger attached with watching the son she gave birth to, sacrificed her happiness for, and gave her everything, turn into a female right before her eyes is paramount to watching death itself. To compound her grief she knows that in all likelihood she will never experience the joy of being a grandmother. She will never see in a grandchild all the hopes and dreams lost on her homosexual son.

As the mother sits back and tries to pinpoint where she went wrong, the father of a daughter, his only child, receives the crushing news that she, daddy's girl, hates men, never intends to marry, and has taken up with a female. He too will never know the delight of becoming a grandfather.

Homosexuality has chopped down many a family tree. The genealogy of thousands of families has been halted because homosexuality revealed as always, Adam and Steve cannot create life.

HOMOSEXUALITY AND MARRIAGE

<u>Marriage</u>: The legal union of a man and woman as husband and wife.

If that is indeed the meaning and has been for thousands of years, the nuptials that fall outside of that definition is the act of an illegal union, isn't it?

<u>Consummate</u>: To bring to completion; to complete a marriage with the first act of sexual intercourse.

<u>Intercourse</u>: Is the act in which the male reproductive organ enters the female reproductive tract.

However, they go on to say that the meaning of intercourse has been broadened in recent years (we know why and by whom) to include anal and oral intercourse. Imagine that; you can now have oral intercourse. Once again homosexuals took a decent word and politicized it to help validate their sex-style. They twisted it and expanded it into something vulgar. Anal intercourse; how ridiculous is that? In order to push a same sex marriage agenda they politicized the word intercourse to make it seem like something two men can actually engage in. Just like the word gay no longer means happy or joyful. It now has a perverted meaning that makes everyone cautious about using it. Homosexuals make up 2-3 % of the U.S. population yet can change the dictionary right before the eyes of the remaining 97%. Maybe we should expand the word stupid to include people who will go along with anything.

Since ancient times intercourse had a declared purpose of reproduction; a pleasurable ritual that led to new life. The Ancient Africans often prayed before engaging in sex. Intercourse cannot take place outside of the woman's womb. No matter how much they claim to love each other two males cannot consummate a marriage. No matter what compromising governing body issues a marriage license, two females cannot consummate a marriage. It is a farce. A penis and a vagina working together, holding the possibility of reproduction from their intercourse, is needed to consummate a marriage. Two people of the same sex cannot have intercourse. Two males sodomizing each other is not anal intercourse, it's simply anal sex; for the sole purpose of pleasure not reproduction.

Two women cannot consummate a marriage. They cannot use vibrators, dildos or any other object to penetrate each other in an attempt to consummate a marriage. There is no life force within an inanimate object. According to tradition and ancient laws, couples who cannot consummate their marriage are not married.

Take a close look at the sexism in the fact that homosexual males claim they can have intercourse; however, the homosexual females cannot have intercourse because they lack a penis. If a penis is the only thing required to have sexual intercourse then a guy can stick his penis into another male's ear and call that intercourse. Any orifice or hole that a penis can be inserted into does not constitute intercourse. That includes an anus. *Intercourse can only be achieved through the birth canal continuum through which life naturally enters this world and take its course; intercourse.*

 European males past and present loved having sex with sheep and other animals. European women still today have sex with animals, including horses. The practice was so widespread they had to make laws to stop it. Is this perversion considered intercourse just because there's a penis involved…. hardly. It still proves the wider point that homosexuality cannot create life only corrupt existing life. Homosexuality can't even create words only corrupt existing words. This is their culture.

Marriage aside, homosexuality limits love and relationships to a physical plain and requires things that enhance and sooth the senses of touch, taste, smell, hearing and sight. However, heterosexuality allows a man and woman to connect on a spiritual plain and invites bonding outside the senses onto a metaphysical cohesion. I've heard homosexual's claims of finding their soul mates. A few months later after the newness of the physical relationship has worn off, the couple separate and each set out to find new soul mates. Serial monogamy (multiple monogamous relationships) keeps people in utter confusion while creating the illusion of morality allowing the practitioner to justify his/her constantly changing sex partners.

A homosexual couple who does manage to stay together ten or twenty years are not soul mates- but kindred spirits. They are individuals who have accepted being abnormal, adjusted to each other's habits, satisfied with their surroundings, and resigned them selves to the routine their relationship entails.

The sanctity of marriage includes protecting words and the true meanings around them. If you change or distort the meaning a word you can no longer use that word in its correct context.

Homosexuals and their Guardians

Guardian: 1.One that guards or protects 2.One that is legally responsible for the care and management of a person or property of an incompetent minor.

I remember watching a horror movie one night and was amazed at how overzealous and uncompromising the human guardians of Dracula's tomb were. They were willing to fight and die for their master's way of life. They themselves were not vampires, yet they guarded and catered to the vampire's every whim. I'm not comparing homosexuality to bloodsucking, but if you think about it, there are a number of similarities. Let's see:

A small group of people who believe they're superior and special, but in order to survive, must physically turn others into what they are. And in order to sleep, they need the protection of guardians and sympathizers who know that bloodsucking is wrong but none-the-less will attack anybody who goes near their master. Hmmm, sound familiar? When I think of a fictionalized vampire, I think of someone draining your body of its positive energy, morality and spirit, because they cannot survive on their own. And once they have changed you into what they are, your positive energy, morality and spirit follows. That's when you start sucking the morality out of others.

In the homosexual world, mothers are the ultimate guardians and protectors of their children's "sex-style." There is no greater champion to the homosexual cause than the mother of a homosexual. If you watch the interviews of women at 'gay' rallies and marches, many of them aren't homosexual, but their children are. They believe that they're helping their children by forcing the world to accept homosexuality instead of trying to help their child correct their perversion. These mothers, when hard pressed, still will not admit that it was their lack of parenting skills that ruined the child's normal development in the first place. Whether it was lax discipline, spoiling, feminist rants, a pedophile babysitter, or total neglect, most roads lead back to the mother.

A father is quick to administer 'tough love' and will cut the child off until they straighten out his/her life; but not the mother. The mother is going to sneak the child food, money and clothes often behind the father's back. In a lot of communities, you can talk about a child's father but insults to the mother usually results in a black eye. That's because the mother as nurturer and protector is highly revered which is why the homosexual child must quickly win over the support of his/her mother before anyone else. A mother's disapproval weighs heavier than a father's shame. Homosexuals will bare the brunt of a father's wrath in order to win the support of the mother. The psychological games played by homosexuals are far reaching and must not be underestimated. They do not mind pitting one parent against the other if it sustains their sexual imperative.

To the homosexual child, the mother is needed and can be counted on for comfort and financial assistance. When things get tough, they need the flexibility to run back to mother. Most fathers of homosexual males cut off all contact and remain bitter and numb toward their sons, while being a lot more understanding of the homosexual daughter. They feel that daughters can be salvaged, straighten out and possibly produce a grandchild, but their son is lost forever. There is no father- son bonding and no real father-son moments to build upon. The thought of the male child's anal submission is too much for most fathers to bare. Some fathers blame themselves for their son's homosexuality, not being available and not being tougher disciplinarians, while a large number of mothers also blame the absentee father for his lack of interest in the extracurricular activities of his son.

My ex-girlfriend Risa use to strongly voice her disapproval of homosexuality, in no uncertain terms. She stated emphatically that 'woman on woman' sex was "nasty, sick behavior." But now that her wayward teenage daughter has been 'turned out' by the 'butch-dyke' female, she seems to be to some degree 'pro-homosexual.' For some unknown reason, she felt that she had to embrace Ciera's conversion to perversion, simply on the basis that it was her child; unbelievable.

I tried to explain to her that a naïve, impressionable nineteen year old being sexually exploited by an older female was no reason to throw in the white towel of surrender. The child needed her help more then ever now. I asked her that if Ciera was a thief, would she think stealing was alright? If Ciera dressed up in leather and was led around by a leash would she advocate bondage or S&M? If Ciera was selling her body, would she favor prostitution? And If Ciera was in the Army, would she support the war in Iraq? You can love the child but hate what they've become. One has nothing to do with the other. If you turn your head away from a problem, you will eventually turn back around to find that it has swelled. Only a fool would go along to get along.

Risa was being reactive to the current situation as opposed to being proactive from the beginning. We'll discuss that later. Either way, under no circumstances, for many of us, surrender is not an option.

Even More Irrational Guardians

In the campaign to win over public opinion, homosexuals will constantly play the 'victim card.' They portray themselves as weak, fragile and just want to be left alone. In actuality, they are the aggressors and/or agitators in most confrontations. It is not enough for the siblings of homosexuals to have to ward off bullies, but 'John Q. Public' has been recruited as a more useful pawn. Homosexuals portray themselves as 'victims' in order to get 'straight' men/women to come to their rescue and ward off challengers.

They manipulate most situations to their advantage by making the opposition a political issue. Homosexual's favorite and most disgusting, shameless political tool is the comparison between their homosexuality and the 'Black Civil Rights Movement'. It's not as if any mocha, mahogany, butter pecan, almond or chocolate flavored man/woman/child could have chosen what color they wanted to be or could hide their dark complexions from the world. Hatred of someone's skin color is far different from hating someone for what they do in the privacy of their bedroom. Unless you open your mouth and tell me, I'd never know what goes on inside your bedroom. No one would ever know a person's sexual orientation unless that person reveals it. However, quite a few Europeans and Negroes buy and sell that ridiculous argument every day.

It took a while for me to understand why homosexuals were opposed to

Clinton's "don't ask, don't tell" military policy. It seemed pretty reasonable to me; I don't go ask you if you're homosexual and you don't come tell me that you are homosexual. There's only one reason why the policy upset homosexuals; they wanted everyone to know what they do in their bedrooms in hopes of recruiting and increasing their homosexual encounters. Unfortunately, parents don't have that option.

This is the process that the condoning parents and guardians of homosexuals go through. See if it applies to you or someone you know:

1) *Rationalize* – <u>try to make sense of it</u>: it's my fault. They were born this way. They can't help it.
2) *Normalize* – <u>It's normal:</u> Everybody's doing it. My neighbors 'gay.' It's all over T.V. and my favorite actor is 'gay.'
3) *Internalize* – <u>they make the doctrine their own and defend it:</u> My son/daughter's gay. I have to defend them. By standing up for homosexuals I'm protecting my child.

Of course there are exceptions to the rule:
*parents who refuse to lose their children to perversion. So they fight for their son/daughter's sanity.
* And let's not forget about the parents who are in denial. They have a don't ask, don't tell, don't see, don't hear and definitely don't want to know policy all of their own.

How do I treat my homosexual Child or loved one?

Carefully, that is your child and you will always love him/her; but carefully. That doesn't mean you must rubber stamp everything they say or do. What parent would tell his child they are right when they are wrong? You have no idea how many arguments I have engaged in with people over the sick actions of their homosexual offspring. If you've noticed when it comes to homosexuality, the younger the child, the more over zealous and over-protective the parent becomes. A mother's natural protective instinct sometimes obstructs her view of right and wrong. I've spoken to many parents who said homosexuality was truly repulsive, until it was their child who got caught up in that world.

Now, they have a whole lot more leniency towards so called 'gays' and venom towards straight people. The ones who are religious are now claiming that God understands and condones their son/daughter's homosexuality. I know mothers who to this day are in denial about their son's rape and murder convictions. "My son wouldn't do anything like that," they maintain. Mothers and fathers often take unconditional love to places it was never meant to go. You can love your child and still fight against his/her perversion.

Far too many parents still do not understand that just because your child was 'turned-out' by the 'homo- thug' or 'butch-dyke' doesn't mean you should simply give up. It also doesn't mean their condition is untreatable or irreversible. Never stop fighting for your child's sanity. But to do this, you must first arm yourself with as much information as possible concerning your child's sexual disorder. Forget about what you think you know; get the facts. As you already found out, running to church and praying to Jesus did not help. You literally went into a building full of homosexual spirits and conjured up other homosexual spirits and asked them for help. Not a good idea.

An important fact: Young girls and boys may be attracted to other young boys and girls of the same sex but their attraction will have nothing to do with sex. Teenagers will sometimes confuse jealous feelings with lustful desires; even anger with hate. At these awkward ages and especially in social settings, teenagers are drawn to other teens that are popular or good looking and they want to emulate them; be close to them. But Homosexual propaganda tries to make them believe they're 'gay' and should explore their feelings. That's where you come in. Think about when you were young and all the awkward feelings, emotions and situations you were in. Their confusion is no different from yours at that age. Confused, runaway, learning disabled, needy and rebellious teenagers make irresistible targets for homosexuals because they're easier to manipulate and control when their parents are unable to communicate with them. Get to know your kids a lot better. In a homosexual environment you may be their only hope.

Right now, the vital information in this book/study is your primary weapon in understanding homosexual behavior. Understanding homosexuality is the key to breaking its grip on your child. Recently, I've noticed a lot of young kids experimenting and playing with homosexuality as if it is a game; it's suddenly cool to be queer. They have no idea how much long term damage they are doing to their minds and bodies. They have no clue as to how strong the homosexual spirits are that they are conjuring up.

First, be patient with your son/daughter, change doesn't happen overnight. Be stern, firm and show tough love. Never bend, because if they are able to bend you, they will break you. Do not invite or accept their homosexual partner openly into your home. By openly, I mean you must show resistance and your true feelings on the matter. That doesn't mean treat them cruelly; you can be cordial without being condoning.

Accept your child, no matter how old, but not his/her sex-style or partner. People with mental disorders need their loved ones close. Expressing your disapproval keeps them cognizant of your mindset. Clearly he/she isn't going to think there's anything wrong with them. They're going to say there's something wrong with you; i.e. homophobic, a prude, embarrassed, or scared of what the neighbors will say.

Winning over the affection or admiration of their partner's parent is crucial to the homosexual. But it is a trap predators use to maintain access to their prey's bodies. Your son/daughter knowing that you accept their homosexual partner also means you're accepting of the things she/he is going to do to your son/daughter's body; no matter how file. Why invite someone over for dinner after they've been abusing your son/daughter's body? What the hell are you thinking about?

Just because your child is an adult doesn't mean they naturally make wise decisions. The decision to let others defile their body is testament to that. And parents who know they have a messed up, screwed up child, should be ashamed to sit next to some innocent victim your son/daughter is corrupting and preying upon. A friend of mine told me that he was warned by his new girlfriend's mother to "get away from her. She'll only bring you down." After a few months he found out exactly what she meant. Too bad more parents aren't that forthcoming about their dishonorable offspring.

Second; never stop analyzing and scrutinizing your child's behavior. It's important to investigate where it came from. Somewhere down the line someone whom you trusted to be around your child violated that trust by means of molestation or indoctrination. Don't blame yourself; find out who, when, and where the psychological transformation took place. Don't blame yourself and give up because it's important to address that specific issue. In doing so you're making your son/daughter acknowledge the genesis of their disorder. A disorder as defined by psychiatrists until homosexuals forced them to change that analysis.

Remember; **homosexuality is all about a sex-style, nothing more.** Why any parent would want to sit across the dinner table from someone who is poking unnatural objects into their child is beyond me. Parents will tell their children not to let their gang banging friends in the house, or their thieving classmates, but homosexuals are just fine. I can't imagine a mother going to the movies with the guy who is sodomizing and probably fisting her son. I can't fathom why a father would have lunch with the 'butch-dyke' who goes against everything he as a man stands for. What kind of love would make a mother sit across the table from the male whose 'tea-bagging' her son?

Is it me, or are you condoning the physical and mental abuse of your own child? Since suicide rates among homosexuals are greater than the general population, shouldn't you be trying to get your child out of danger? Shouldn't you be trying to keep him from wearing a diaper? Shouldn't you be trying to keep her from hating men and dressing like a man? There is substantial evidence proving that homosexuality presents significant danger to a person's psychological health (see statistics). That said, why would any parent risk losing their child by spoiling him/her and submitting to their harmful, lustful desires? It's a fine line between parenting and enabling. If you don't know where to draw the line, then you've probably already crossed it.

Homosexuals and Children

If you want to control or destroy a society, start with its children. Everybody knows that. The selfish nature of homosexuality has no mercy on the evolving minds of children. Weather adopted or engineered, the children of homosexuals are almost certainly scarred for life. This is unavoidable. The statistics that involve single parent households are irrefutable and troubling enough. But a household with same sex parents seems to only be good for financial mobility, not emotional stability, and suits the fantasy of that adoptive parent, not the development of the child. (My section of 'Statistics' will tell the tale).

There are only a few reasons why homosexuals want children and lately it seems like a desperate urgency. Why do homosexuals want to get their hands on children so badly? Why would a homosexual want a child? Since homosexuality gained the political statue it enjoys today, homosexuals have always screamed, "I was born this way, I can't help I", or "this is how God made me." By saying these things, they admit that their behavior is not normal, therefore, they are abnormal. Why would a person who admits to be abnormal want to adopt a child? Simple; through that child, their legacy of homosexuality can live on. That child will not only be homosexual friendly, but quite possibly queer. A straight couple will live on through their children. In a lot of ways, parent's dreams, goals and values live on in through their children. A homosexual couple would like to leave something behind when they die as well; their legacy of homosexuality.

In as much as heterosexual parent's birth children to love, share and wean into their image, homosexuals aspire the same things. The same values about life and love "straight" (as opposed to crooked I guess) parents instill into their children, homosexual parents want to instill same -sex happiness and a strange form of gender equality: **Mother is not mother, father is not father but are equal in structure and perform the same functions within the nuclear family**. They wish to rear a child into their image. The joy that a heterosexual couple feels the day their child takes its first steps is the same joy some homosexual couples feel the day their child says "guess what, I'm gay."

As many homosexuals age, they have begun to realize that the loss of genealogy due to their homosexuality will leave them emotionally impaired. They will have no one to rely on or to take care of them when they're old and unable. They will have no one to leave their money, homes or property to when they die. Although most homosexuals have family or extended family, these relatives usually want little if anything to do with them. So to offset that loss of family and connection, they work tirelessly to get their hands on children. They exert enormous effort into crafting legislation and propaganda geared towards 'gay marriage' and adoption. Being legally recognized as a married couple with all the amenities awarded straight couples, they become one step closer to adoption.

There is an abundance of hard to place children within the child welfare system. Some say that within the system, it now comes down to a choice between parents or no parents. It seems homosexual couples are willing to take the most troubled or ill children into their homes; why, because it is a secret strategy to obtain the rights and benefits of a normal married couple. It's politics as usual. No matter what anybody says this is social engineering. If you take an honest look at the effects single parenting and divorce has on a child the decision is clear; children need to grow up in a two parent, mother and father environment. They need both male and female role models. Since 85% of children with behavioral problems and who end up in prison come from fatherless homes, there is obviously a problem.

Lesbian couples getting artificial insemination have little regard for the child but only think that a new baby will make them happy and keep them bonded forever. But there can be no balance within that house hold. God forbid if the child wants to meet his biological father someday. A lesbian housekeeper in the Ocean View section of Norfolk, Virginia, an area known for drugs, prostitution, homosexuality, transients, interracial couples, gangs and shootings, told me that her six year old son, calls her homosexual, 'butch-dyke' partner, 'daddy.' Now picture that; a six year old Black boy growing up in an already hostile environment, being raised by two females, is encouraged to call his mother's masculine looking female partner, 'daddy.' The duality needed for a female who hates men but wants to be a man and raise a boy into manhood is simply unobtainable. It is the ultimate in confusion. Between the obtrusive male bashing, feminine rhetoric and emasculation, that poor boy doesn't stand a chance. The goal of the 'butch-dyke' is to make her female presence stronger than any male.

Not to mention that statistics prove that homosexual relationships, male and female, are shorter than the life span of a fruit fly. Of course, that is do to the lack of a spiritual connection a same sex sex-style precludes. A mother encouraging her son to call her sexual partner 'daddy' may serve to stroke the 'butch-dyke's' ego, but it absolutely destroys the developing mind of the young male. He will not concede the proper role in life nature has designated him to play. He mixes and matches masculine and feminine values, principles and even mannerisms. The boy will grow up with an distorted view of social and sexual relationships. The 'butch-dyke' may feel she's a hero in a lesbian relationship by stepping up to fill a man's shoes.

But her being referred to as 'Daddy' is completely self-serving. The 'butch-dyke' does this to enhance her presence within the household and gives the boy's mother more of a reason to be dependant upon her; hence keeping her around. The 'butch-dyke' creates the illusion of a 'father-son' connection between herself and the growing boy; therefore, her presence and power within the household becomes indispensable. She's made to feel important. But be sure, there can be no father/son moments between them; only the confusion of a young male to older female sentiment. A female can have male tendencies and adopt male mannerisms but her information is contrived and patterned after the men she sees at work or on television.

She copies and internalizes stereotypes that most men themselves don't like; that include her walk, her dress, her speech and huge bravado. Although pretending to be a man, a woman is capable of only maternal instincts not paternal instincts. Therefore, her knowledge and concepts for raising a boy into manhood are not intuitive but the flawed guesswork of an imitator; a bootleg copy of a man. Once again, it is the selfishness of homosexuality that puts the needs of the homosexual ahead of the child.

Earlier I stated the housekeeper's occupation and environment for a reason. First, poverty very well may have skewed the housekeeper's vision as to the people she allowed into her son's life. A lot of times, folks who live in impoverished conditions are so focused on surviving week to week that they ignore all the stoplights and warning signs they pass. Food, shelter, transportation, and a steady paycheck become all that matters. They rationalize abhorrent behavior because the end justifies the means. Second, and again, environment can dictate lifestyle. Surviving in a hostile environment without a man, for whatever reason, can push a female in the direction of a man-like substitute. The unnatural state of adults without mates creates a nagging void.

I feel sorry for all young kids growing up without a father, as I did for this boy. And God forbid if this boy's father should one day return, intent on taking his proper place in his son's life, he will undoubtedly be met with unbelievable hostility and opposition. I'm not saying a woman can't raise a man. It has been done. They do what they have to. But you can brush your teeth with your finger instead of a toothbrush, that doesn't make it a good idea. A boy being raised without a father is almost always missing a balance. It's like making a cake without all the ingredients. To evolve into a complete, well-rounded man, he, on his own, will have to find the missing ingredients that will give him this balance.

Believe it or not, the housekeeper also said that if one day her son announced that he was 'gay,' she would be perfectly alright with it. Of course, that is a patented answer given by homosexuals the world over. But her answer was straight bullshit. I guaranty you that if the housekeeper was forced to choose between witnessing her son bend over, spread his butt cheeks and be sodomized by another male or watch him spread the legs of a young woman and engage in natural, heterosexual intercourse, she would unquestionably choose the latter.

Two men and a little Boy

And I am not talking about a television show. There isn't much to be said here except; Why would homosexual males want to adopt a little boy? Since you read the section called 'Born that way', then you are fully aware of the ramifications of a homosexual male being in close quarters with young boys, more less adopting them. By definition being a homosexual male says you're rejecting being a man yourself. What can you possibly teach a young male child?

Did you know that 40 years old was the average age of a pedophile? Let's examine some facts. Remember, in their book 'After the Ball......' Homosexual authors Kirk and Madsen tells us that "most gays are single minded predators...fixated on youth and physical beauty alone....when it comes to the old and ugly gays, they are the real queer bashers....they are cynical about love ....unattractive gay men find it nearly impossible to find a friend, let alone a lover...."

The reason why there are so many pedophiles is because once homosexuals reach a certain age, nobody wants them. So they have no choice but to prey on little boys or girls; those who are the weakest among us. Homosexuals with power, money and influence are usually the only ones who are able to lure the younger and attractive homosexuals because of their social status and the material wealth they're able to heap upon them. Young boys have always been the targets of older, homosexual males.

As a general rule of thumb, wherever there are groups or gatherings of little boys or young boys, there are homosexual pedophiles nearby. All of whom are in positions of authority. There should never be a question as to if there's a pedophile nearby, the question should always be; which one of these adult males is the pedophile and how can I stop him? It's just that simple. The Boy Scouts 'pervert files' as they've been called, are further proof of that.

Adolescent boys who were abused by men are up to seven times more likely to identify themselves as homosexual or bisexual. At the Connecticut Correctional Institution, for example, Clinical Psychologist A. Nichols Groth, director of the sex offender program said 85% of the pedophiles were themselves sexually assaulted as youths. So many homosexual males had their own same-sex encounters (rape) with an adult while they themselves were children. Adoption simply shows they intend to pass that trauma on. Two men and a little boy; God I hope not.

Homosexuals and child rearing

The most important part of this daily routine we call life is our children. No matter what color you are, how poor, uneducated, religious, or handicapped, we will do anything for our children. No matter where we were going or how screwed up our lives were before they arrived, once we saw their faces, we immediately changed our outlook, our destination and our lives. We had to straighten up because it's all about them now. That's how it was for most of us anyway. We live for our children and sometimes through our children. They are our future. Nothing compares to their happiness and well-being. The most fundamental aspect of being a parent is tending to the stability and proper development of our children. One immediate act a parent performs when their children reaches the age of reason is teaching them values; telling them **'yes'** and **'no'** and the consequences that are the result of their choices. These two very simple words are the foundation of our children learning discipline.

Without discipline, our children will not respect boundaries, are unable to tell themselves **'no'** and find themselves open to every drug, stimulant, indoctrination and perversion life will send their way. There is no debate, even among homosexuals as to whether or not they respect boundaries; they do not. Statistically, homosexuals as a group have very little discipline. Selfish, individualistic, disrespectful, aggressive, remorseless behavior dominates their culture. The homosexual idea of discipline is **'if it feels good, do it.'** Homosexuality, because of its inability to build off spirituality must exist off physiology. Therefore, its very commonplace for homosexuals to focus on themselves and their individual wants than on the needs of children.

Homosexuality in and of itself is not a natural state. Homosexuals will tell you as much, therefore the opposite of natural is unnatural. Homosexual parents are by default expecting their children to unconditionally accept something that is unnatural even to them, as well as accepting all the problems that surround people living in an unnatural state- emotionally, physically and mentally. Of course homosexuals will tell you that they are great parents, but by forcing children to reconcile between their homosexual parents and the heterosexual influences of everyone else, is damaging and creates a harmful internal struggle within the child. These children don't develop naturally because they're wedged between their heterosexual friends and peers who disagree with their parent's homosexual world. The child's life is now filled with propaganda, distortions, conflicts, taunts, fights and perverse ideologies. For a homosexual to force a child, especially an adolescent in the confusing developmental stages of his/her life, to accept perversion (go back and look up the definition of perversion) as a lifestyle is once again, self serving.

Think about your own parents getting a divorce and asking you to choose which of them you wanted to live with. Can you imagine the pressure and guilt you'd be feeling? That is the ultimatum given to the children of homosexuals. They are forced into a battle between the 3% of Americans who are homosexual or so-called 'homosexual friendly', and the 97% their parents are constantly at odds with. How is this good parenting? Why would anyone want to put children in the middle of a conflict they've created for themselves? Does it make sense? No. But it serves the homosexual agenda, gives the illusion of a normal family, creates a new generation of homosexuals where none existed, and builds a bridge for homosexual legislation to cross over.

Their willingness to drag children into their own psychological and emotional hell should automatically disqualify homosexuals from the adoption process. But it doesn't. Since we all know that child rape is the number one cause of homosexuality, then why would homosexual parents expose their children to their
homosexual friends? "My friends would never do anything like that," is what they'll say. However, that goes against every single solitary study that has ever been conducted. The fact that most sexual assaults are committed by someone the victim knows is proof of that. Perversion has no friends. **Here's your valid distinction between heterosexual and homosexual adoption:**
In this study, I have found that the children of homosexuals overwhelmingly shared the same identical issues surrounding their parent's sex-styles.
The *children of homosexual parents*:
1 *Are embarrassed by their parents and teased and taunted by their peers*
2 *Often only hang with each other because they feel they are the only ones who understand what the other is going through*
3 *Carry around guilt and fear of someone finding out*
4 *Grow up wondering if they are going to be 'gay' or if they are already 'gay' and don't know it or if their parents' homosexuality was somehow passed on to them*
5 *Were always used as tokens to show the world how normal homosexuals were*

This study also revealed that lesbian parents constantly bash men(even sub-consciously), change partners just when their children have finally gotten to know their mate, constantly indoctrinate their children with homosexual propaganda, and too often choose partners who view the older male children as a threat. The children of homosexuals are also three times more likely to be homosexual then children with heterosexual parents.

Spoiled Children

"Spoiled children are more easily homosexualized and effeminized because they only see the things that they want...People who are desperate for attention will accept it from anyone. It is an addiction. And whoever supplies the drug, provides the food, shelter and clothing, gives the attention, can lead the receiver wherever s/he or it wants the receiver to go." Baruti p. 398

A lot of spoiled children turn into adults who need to be taken care of. In knowing this, homosexuals use materialism as a ploy to trap much younger victims. And I say victim because anyone who falls prey to a predator is exactly that. Spoiled young women are especially vulnerable to predatory older females who'll quickly whisper "you don't have to worry about nothing; I'll take care of you," into their ready ear. The promise of luxury and escape from home has left many a young woman's life a confused mess. Predatory homosexuals understand the importance of psychology on the heterosexual mind.

After luring the financially dependent young woman from the constraints of her family, the homosexual female easily becomes the sole source of the materialistic young woman's income and survival. Once away from home, the homosexual will invoke the fear of removing her materialistic trinkets, clothes, car, and shelter to keep the spoiled young woman in 'check.' Parents with female children must understand this. In an attempt to keep your child, the so called 'butch-dyke' must exercise control mentally, emotionally and sexually. Never at any time underestimate the aggressive tendencies of the 'butch-dyke.'

If the 'butch-dyke' doesn't feel accepted in your family, she will begin the process of distancing/ then separating you from your child. It is a maneuver that most homosexuals use, male and female, to secure the survival of their relationship to your child. Relationship isolation is nothing new to heterosexual couples, but in homosexual couples, it is seldom discussed because the parents naturally assume it is their child choosing to keep his/her distance from them versus the psychological manipulation of his/her homosexual partner.

Quite a few psychological games must be played in order to maintain her new homosexual relationship with your previously straight child, if possible, moving away then immersing your kid in her homosexual world; i.e. 'gay' clubs, friends and functions. The constant scrutiny of public opinion and the internal conflict to legitimize an abnormal relationship in a world governed by normal heterosexuals keeps many 'butch-dykes' on the edge of their seat. In other words, it would not be a stretch to say that a large portion of 'butch-dykes' live in constant fear of losing a newly turned partner to a straight male.

That's why contact with ex-boyfriends, 'baby's daddies' and workplace males is closely monitored and/or prohibited. And therefore is often overcompensated by the 'butch-dykes' psychological manifestations/expressions in the forms of bravado, flamboyance, money and precautionary anger. Money and the complimentary use of material objects serve the purpose of control. These are defense mechanisms. That said, relationships amongst poor or working class homosexuals who don't have the resources to run for the hills or buy influence during times of adversity, must use anger or pity to maintain relationships. Newly turned partners begin to think of themselves as the protector or 'only friend' of the misunderstood 'butch-dyke.' It is the pity they require from their partner and/or heterosexual 'big brothers or sisters' who find them too weak to defend themselves against straight males. Never underestimate the effectiveness of pity.

Always Challenge Words

Always challenge words, phrases and accusations; always.

Alright everybody here's our new word list:

homophobic	*straight*
bi-sexual	*civil rights*
oral intercourse	*gay-bashing*
anal intercourse	*gay*

Did you ever sit back and ponder how powerful a thought can become? Our most basic thoughts come alive every day.
Our thoughts become words and our words become deeds and our deeds are physical manifestations of our thoughts. It is a pattern we rarely notice. For better or worse, every day, we speak thousands of thoughts into existence. We even know how to transmit these thoughts to others by the speaking of words. That lie about 'sticks and stones may break my bones but words will never hurt me' is not true. Words hurt. Words create, words resonate, words invoke.

Trigger words: words specifically used to trigger an emotional response.

The repeated and misguided use of trigger words by any group can give undue power and relevance to the most benign words in the English language. At the same time, the misuse and misinterpretation of harmless words by any group can change the intended meaning altogether. In order to give words relevance and authority, trigger words must be constantly repeated. They must affect people on a visceral level. Trigger words must have an emotional attachment that invokes an immediate emotional response; crying, anger, hostility, immobility, fear, etc.

Take for instance; the words 'civil rights.' When someone says "civil rights," we immediately think about the 1960's, segregation, boycotts, riots, marches and Martin Luther King, Jr. That's because the 1960's was the focal point of emotional trauma that surrounded those words and where the environment aptly reflected their constant and repeated use. It became ingrained in our subconscious. The words 'civil rights' have deep sentiment amongst Blacks. Whenever we hear or read about someone getting their civil rights violated, we immediately sit up and listen. No matter what we are doing, we want to hear what's happened.

 Homosexuals know this. That's why they constantly try to connect their own ostracism by heterosexual America to Black oppression and the civil rights movement. Whenever someone says the words 'civil rights,' they want Blacks and sympathetic Whites to think about homosexuals. By standing on the backs of African-Americans who have suffered, bled and died, homosexuals are shamelessly trying to fulfill their same- sex agenda.

I don't know one single black man/woman who chose what color they were born or the family they were born into. Homosexuals have the luxury of keeping their sexual orientation private thereby making their business their business. But they do not. Mind games are synonymous with homosexuals. Since they have no shame or reservations about building a political platform off the sacrifice or death and suffering of so called 'minorities,' why then should anyone have any hesitations about pulling such a platform down?

Homosexual oppression is a lie built upon lies. Homosexuals have always been amongst the most powerful, privileged and ruling classes; freely using the world and everyone in it as their personal play things. From clergymen in confessionals to entire cities and states; Greece, Rome, Holland, and San Francisco, they've always frequented open sex clubs, gay night clubs, steam rooms, even in prison, homosexuals aren't quarantined but are free to prey upon the rest of the population. They've been allowed to have civil unions and gather without physical violence in parks. They've been performing sex acts on each other in bathrooms all across this country, until children and others became exposed to their public sex exhibitions, forcing the police to crack down.

J. Edger Hoover, Liberace and Rock Hudson enjoyed their homosexual lifestyles their entire lives. They lived out their homosexual fantasies with total impunity. It wasn't until homosexuals decided to tell their neighbors and indoctrinate their children that the real war began. The lengths homosexuals will go to validate their sex-style is sometimes frightening.

Homosexuals only start screaming their being oppressed when they can't have their way or are not allowed to do as they please, unabated. By telling a homosexual 'no,' you are creating boundaries they feel do not and should not apply to them. And they will never be happy until they have the unrestricted power they crave.

They envision a world where homosexuality is normal, where young boys and girls can be freely pursued without fear of indictment, condemnation or incarceration. They envision a world where heterosexual men and women can be approached freely on the streets, touched and groped without fear, violence or recourse. Homosexuals will not stop until men and women are able to have same sex marriages and privileges, and fathers will marry daughters and sons will marry their biological mothers. Don't say it's not possible. Perversion knows no boundaries. One only need look no further then Greece or Rome to see homosexual societies in ruins.

That is why we must monitor and understand the power of words; words like gay-bashing. Homosexuals will label any book, letter, movie, essay, commentary or editorial that does not champion their agenda as gay-bashing; especially this book. Any athlete or television personality who speaks out against homosexuality faces serious financial ruin. To voice one's opinion on any social issues is not bashing. To speak out against any perversion is a right you should hold sacred. Fact is there's no such thing as 'gay-bashing.' It is a desperate attempt to silence descent. It is a political term that was constantly repeated and eventually caught on.

While we're talking about the word 'gay,' let's examine its true political meaning. Many years ago, according to the dictionary 'gay' was a word that meant merry, playful and happy, until homosexuals hijacked it and put a psychological twist on it. Their true intent was to connect their queer behavior with the word, 'gay,' therefore when you think of homosexuals, you think of happy, playful and merry people instead of a male sodomizing another male. The word 'gay' has been perverted so that it not only includes this new homosexual reference in the dictionary, but anyone who uses the term these days must be careful or else a basic conversation can easily be misconstrued. You no longer can refer to a happy person or your playful, merry child as 'gay,' because the very first thing every one will think about is homosexuality; sad.

Straight was a term coined by homosexuals and bestowed upon non-homosexuals of whom they were hoping to 'turn out.' But once people figured out that in order to be called 'straight,' the person using the term was by default 'crooked,' they soon refrained from using the word. A homosexual admitting that they are in fact 'crooked,' is truly an accurate self analysis.

'Homophobic' is the most political and ill considered word ever invented. A 'phobia' by definition is an unnatural fear of something. But no one fears homosexuals, their lifestyle or sex-style. It is only their unethical political tactics that get people alarmed. Yet, anyone who vocally disagrees with homosexuality is labeled 'homophobic.' This strategy allows homosexuals to launch continuous verbal attacks on their enemies and deceive the public into taking their side. The public begins to think the person accused of having this imaginary 'Phobia' needs counseling instead of the homosexual. It also aids homosexuals in preventing heterosexuals from adequately defending themselves by making the accused appear unreasonable and mean-spirited.

Bi-sexual is a term coined by homosexuals who were ashamed to say they were homosexual. To say someone goes "both ways" means they are either
a.) absolutely confused, cannot commit, or
b.) views their relationships through a physical prism by which to indulge their sexual gratifications and perversions.

There is no such thing as 'bi-sexual'; just further confusion for homosexuals as they attempt to add a layer of legitimacy to their cause. Terms like transsexual, transvestite, and transgender all confuse people into thinking there's more to homosexuality then meets the eye; layers of rationalizations meant to confuse an uneducated public. Again, it helps assist in legislation that will lead to legalization.

'Anal intercourse' doesn't exist. And 'Oral intercourse' is the most ridiculous word a homosexual ever came up with. More proof that people without spirituality will go to any length to manufacture it. Oral sex is clearly a sex act and for many the equivalent of foreplay. One male ingesting the semen of another does not change that fact. Seamen as a life giving force, wasn't intended for the oral or anal cavity. Intercourse was designed by nature to be a consensual act between a man and woman that not only felt very pleasurable but was for the function of procreating. In fact, some Africans cultures prayed before having intercourse.

For the sleeping public to allow homosexuals to corrupt an almost sacred word like 'intercourse' is unfathomable. Why are heterosexuals being pulled into this homosexual world of make believe and street corner psychology? Because they do not see any harm the perverting of words will do to their children twenty-five or fifty years from now. The success homosexuals are having convincing the world that marriage can be between people of the same sex is a troubling testament to that.

We have to take heed of the power in our words. They represent us as much as any picture. As a most astute solution, we are obligated to always challenge words, phrases and accusations; always. Never let a homosexual's words or attacks go unchallenged. We must no longer submit and be pulled into the homosexual's make believe world. We must all stay firmly planted in reality.

First, the term 'gay' should be stricken from every heterosexual's vocabulary and replaced by its predecessor; homosexual. Now that you are aware of its true political meaning, you should no longer want to use it anyway. You can also replace the word 'gay' with the term 'queer.' Not only is it a more accurate term describing homosexuality, but years ago, queer was the word homosexuals used to describe each other. Another interesting word I never understood is 'straight.' Why did homosexuals refer to non-homosexuals as 'straight?' I guess in the early days they truly knew that they had psychological problems. In order to categorize any group of people as "straight" the opposing group would by default be "crooked," right? This re-enforces your position and brings the person who is 'crooked' under much needed scrutiny. Many homosexuals have come to realize they're calling themselves "crooked" by labeling everybody else as 'straight,' so they no longer use it. No one wants to be thought of as 'crooked' no mater how true it is.

Whenever anyone is said to be 'homophobic' always clarify the term. Since you now understand that there's no such thing, you're prepared to state the facts. Explain the political significance to others who do not. Of course, this includes other mis-used homosexual terms like 'gay-bashing,' 'bi-sexual' and "anal or oral intercourse." We must never shrink from our responsibility to protect and teach our children or alert the public.

Gay sensitivity training is now being mandated in colleges and schools all Across America. In other words, if you do not take the homosexual propaganda courses, often given by homosexuals or their mothers, at some point during your studies, you will not receive your degree or diploma. This far reaching conspiracy is to get you acquainted, tolerant and accepting of homosexuality before you go out into the world. Such courses use to be voluntary. Now it's mandatory with consequences if you don't comply. Notice these aren't classes on being sensitive to people who are handicapped or people who have religious differences, its homosexuality 101. And its coming to a school near you.

The Spirit of Homosexuality

There's an energy field around this planet. You can't see it or touch it but its there. Spiritual energy is real. It is all around us. You can feel energy in sports arenas. Sometimes it is the only thing that makes a losing team win. You can literally feel the energy at pep rallies and rock concerts. You can especially feel energy within the walls of churches. Every weekend churches emit great masses of energy around the world with their singing, dancing, hugging, joining hands and praying.

To fully grasp the effects of negative energy you must first accept that homosexuality is a living, breathing entity; an entity that must feed off a weak society. Until you understand that, you will never figure out your enemy. Yes, homosexuality is your enemy. It is society's longstanding enemy. It is nature's enemy, therefore it is your enemy. Realize that to a small, irrational group of people homosexuality is their god. They will do anything to protect, feed and worship their god. I know that this is a difficult concept for those of you who do not understand metaphysics. Open your third eye so that it may reveal an inescapable truth. Homosexuals fight for homosexuality in the same way brainwashed Christians fight for Christ. They are overzealous, relentless, blind and indoctrinated to harbor a "take no prisoners" attitude when it comes to serving their god. They both intend to convert you by any means necessary. And until you face the fact that homosexuals are at war with nature (our mother) you are ill prepared to fight. Therefore you or someone you know is bound to become a mental or physical casualty of their indoctrination.

You therefore have become a soldier by default. Christians say they are guided by an entity they call the 'holy spirit'. Every week in Unisom they think, speak and call his name and by doing so they invoke his spirit. It travels among them. Until recently the world had yet to understand that they (homosexuals) also have created an entity of homosexuality. Everyday homosexuals invoke a dangerous, perverse spirit as ancient as Greece itself. It travels amongst them. And when they collectively speak and gather they give that homosexual entity power. It is how the spirit of homosexuality has become so strong and it is why it must be defeated.

Can Homosexuality Be Changed?

First and foremost, I'll reference the highly regarded **Archives of Sexual Behavior** which claims that of homosexuals who underwent 'reparative therapy' 78% of males and 95% of females turned 'straight'. The **Laumann Study** (1994) found that homosexuality was not a 'stable trait.' Therefore change is not impossible but optional. In **U.S. News & World Report**, May 24, 1993 it says; "studies indicate that **psychotherapy** is an effective treatment for people suffering from emotional or mental problems." The main focus of psychotherapy is getting the patient to rethink the relationship between the body and mind. This therapy is meant to change destructive behavior patterns which will reduce anxiety, discourse and pain."

In the **USA Today** March 2008 issue Delores T. Puterbaugh agrees with **psychotherapy** from professionals; not family or friends. "A therapist discerns symptoms of serious emotional distress from situational unhappiness, understands human development (or the lack thereof) across the lifespan, and has other professional skills… a therapist (generally) does not have ulterior motives, is disinterested, and not self serving in the relationship, whereas a spouse may be motivated to appease you, and family members may be invested in the status Quo."

Social Therapy is learning to associate with the positive and disassociate with the negative. **Nutritional Therapy** is guarding your mind and body against toxins not conducive to healthy living and normal thinking.

But again; can homosexuality be changed?

YES, according to *Dr. Llaila Afrika*- 'The American Psychiatric Association labels excessive eating as a disease but homosexuality as normal; how's that possible? Homosexuality must be treated on several different levels simultaneously. It is mandatory to detoxify the body; juices and herbs to steady the nerves and balance hormone levels (depending on the individual, even estrogen), stay away from milk and dairy products because they are acidic. Then you must also treat the addictive behavior and thoughts; deal with the addictive emotions that lead to physical indulgence. But remember, in treating homosexuality the patient needs the support of family and friends, a mentor, elders, attend study groups, and men's groups. A complete reorientation of their social behavior must take place. For example; don't watch videos, movies or read magazines that reinforce homosexuality. At the same time the homosexual's chemical cravings must be treated because homosexuals crave certain behaviors as well as display symptoms; having sex without the urge or desire, going on sex binges and using sex to medicate themselves when feeling hurt, angry or frustrated. *It is a full court press rehabilitation process.*' (Italics mine)

Can Homosexuality Be Changed?

YES, according to Dr. Paul Cameron of the Family Research Institute-
"Clearly the easier problem to eliminate is homosexual behavior; just as many heterosexuals control their desires to engage in premarital or extramarital sex, so some with homosexual desires discipline themselves to abstain from homosexual contact."

Can Homosexuality Be Changed?

YES, according to Joseph Nicolosi, Ph.D. - in his book 'Reparative Therapy of Male Homosexuality'. "The word homosexual names an aspect of such a man's Psychological condition. But he is not gay. "GAY" describes a contemporary socio-political identity and lifestyle which such a man will never claim. Therefore, I call him a "non-gay homosexual"….the non-gay homosexual is a man who experiences a split between his value system and his sexual orientation. He is fundamentally identified with the heterosexual pattern of life. The non-gay homosexual feels his personal progress to be deeply encumbered and by his same-sex attractions. He usually holds conservative values, is identified with a religious tradition, and holds no deep resentments towards Judeo- Christian teachings on homosexuality. In fact he most likely finds them reinforcing and supportive of his struggle. Reparative therapy works off the premise that males having homosexual relations seek encouragement and emotional intimacy from other males as a means of repairing their sense of masculinity that was damaged due to their failure to bond with their fathers. And women are subconsciously looking for the perfect mother in their lesbian relations.

Can Homosexuality Be Changed?

YES, GOD I HOPE SO, according to Xavier James-
Once a person has made up his/ her mind to walk away from homosexuality and lead a heterosexual life, self discipline is crucial to their success. Just like an alcoholic must stay away from bars, homosexuals must be fully aware of their triggers- things that make them regress; 'gay' bars and parties, homosexual propaganda, any and all pornography. That includes movies with violence in relation to sex. Remember, sadomasochism, and all violence connected with sex is abnormal. People may say they're just being kinky but it's actually a sickness. If the only way you can become aroused or achieve an orgasm is by beating, hitting, and chocking someone or having someone choking and beating on you, there's a serious problem. Believe me, there's a difference between getting freaky and getting tortured.

 Contrary to popular belief sex and violence do not go together. When you meet a person who's into violent sex it's usually the result of some past abuse. This person remembers their abuse, identifies with their abuser (in a lot of cases admires their abuser) normalizes the abuse and incorporates it as a part of their own sexual activities. It is a social construct just like homosexuality. And nine times out of ten if you look into that person's past, you'll find childhood or adolescent abuse. Go out and research and contact former homosexuals and ask them how they were able to change. Some of them may even credit the church or religion and that's fine, whatever works for you. Fact is some form of spirituality is ultimately needed to put you on the right track and keep you on the right path.

The world would view homosexuality differently if it knew this condition was preventable and reversible. But instead, society encourages this self destructive behavior because they've been programmed to believe it's hereditary. The political, social and financial benefits for those who promote this myth have been bountiful. For many it's yielded a lifetime of privilege, preferential treatment, tax free, residual incomes and social status. For others it's yielded this so called 'sexual freedom', and fulfilled their need to be seen and feel special about themselves.

Those Vital Statistics

"A homosexual's lifespan is an average 24 years shorter than that of a heterosexual."
-Family Research Institute, 2000

When I first read the above statement I immediately thought about all the known homosexuals in the small Virginia town I grew up in. It was the kind of place where everyone knew each other. The kind of place where you could sneeze and before dark people on the other side of town knew you had a cold. Let's see, there was *Terrance* who was a well known cook in Suffolk. He was killed a few of years ago allegedly by a guy who he'd threatened to tell his wife about their relationship. I think he was around 50. I remember a homosexual named *Antwan* whom it was said could have a bowel movement standing upright without even straining. In the mid 80's he was pushed through a department store window as an unfortunate victim of a hate crime. That didn't kill him. However, several years later he was found dead in an abandoned house; murdered. I think he was in his mid 30's. I remember a homosexual male named *Hank* used to live next door to my grandmother. He also died in the mid 90's. Folks said he had cancer but I don't know. Then there was this red head prostitute from New York, I think, who moved to Suffolk to lay low. He had AIDS. I know because the Suffolk police were going around telling people to watch out for him. He died a few years after moving to Suffolk. And trust me it wasn't from boredom. Then there was 6'1, 200 plus pounds, forty- something year old *Lavern* whom the police sprayed with pepper spray during a traffic altercation. He hyperventilated and died. I think he was in his early forties. In Norfolk around 1993 I remember a young homo-thug out in the Young's Park housing projects killed a homosexual male who had allegedly given him A.I.D.S. The killer and victim were both in their twenties.

As it seems every homosexual male I'd heard of when I was young most certainly died early. Suddenly, this whole homosexual lifespan thing made since. Sit back and think about all the homosexuals you've known in your life and where they are today. It's clear: homosexual conduct reduces life expectancy. Weather they were abusing their bodies from the inside or allowing someone else to abuse their bodies from the outside; the results were permanent. Homosexuals will undoubtedly argue that in a number of cases hate crime was the cause of death and America's attitudes towards them causes this disparity, therefore the statistics are flawed. However, the statistics are the result of adding up homosexual deaths. Like it or not a homosexual sex-style led to the untimely deaths. If these males were not homosexual the violent situations surrounding their deaths probably would not have occurred.

But check this out; in The American Public Health Association 133-137, <u>Jan 2009,</u> doctors Morten Frisch,MD, PHD, DSC(med) and Henrick Bronnum-Hansen,MSC concluded:

"Despite recent marked reduction in mortality among gay men, Danish men and women in same sex marriages still have mortality rates that exceed those of general populations…"

Homosexual accepting societies like Norway, Canada and Denmark where so called 'gay bashing' and 'discrimination' is not a problem still sights homosexuals die significantly sooner then the rest of the population. Imagine that. Even The Kazmann report stated that only 1% of homosexuals live past age 65. That's one hell of a statistic to ignore. Why are married/single homosexual males and females still dying early even when they live in the most pristine homosexual environments and societies on earth? Well it's because of the unnatural spiritual energy that surrounds them. A homosexual relationship induces certain spiritual death. And the human body cannot live without its spirit. The male/female spirits need each other to exist. It is one of nature's inescapable laws. Ying and Yang cannot be separated. They are like interlocking chains.

A hostile environment is but one cause in the short lifespan of homosexuals. And in far too many cases it is an atmosphere they themselves had created. I use to live downstairs from a young handicapped homosexual who went by the nick name 'Joe.' Joe was the standard narcissistic type of homosexual who not only used his disability to get away with abhorrent behavior but he displayed disrespect for everything and everybody that happened into his zone. Anything was subject to come out of his mouth or go into his mouth. He was unemployed and probably unemployable which permitted him to have parties all hours of the night with no regard for any of his neighbors. The people who went in and out of his apartment were some of the foulest individuals park place had to offer. Thieves, prostitutes, drug dealers, drug addicts, gang bangers and 'wanna' be pimps were an everyday scene at his place.

One Saturday evening around 5:30 pm a young, intoxicated male named Tim came to confront a group of boys who'd gathered out front of our building. One of them had said Tim was gay. Tim swore on everything he loved to beat down anyone who'd said he'd engaged in anal sex with Joe. It came to light that Tim had been frequenting the apartment of my homosexual neighbor and word of his visits had circulated throughout the neighborhood. Now, apparently his reputation, status and manhood were in question among his peers. Tim called Joe outside to verbally verify that the two of them were not having anal sex. Of course Tim posed the question in a more vulgar form but for you I've rephrased it. Unfortunately, the six, ten and fourteen year old children who filled the streets that hot summer afternoon had no recourse and were forced to witness this sick spectacle. Needless to say in front of twenty-five plus spectators, mostly children, homosexual Joe laughingly denied any sex acts took place. For Tim's sake, what else was he going to say? While his mouth was saying 'no' the look on Joes snide face was saying 'yes.'

But the question remained; why would a heterosexual male spend so much time in the company of a homosexual male? Short answer; they're both queer. A short time after that incident someone burned a fireball in front of Joe's door. Soon after that a group of females came by wanting to fight Joe and threatened to shoot up his place. My family and I lived downstairs so of course I was concerned. A week after that one of Joe's friends pulled a gun on a neighbor. That entire year it was one incident after another. The police visits or threats from the landlord did little to change Joe's behavior.

The reason I chose to tell you about my homosexual, former neighbor Joe is because when discussing the short lifespan of homosexuals one must keep in mind a lifestyle filled with unnecessary drama and negative karma. Many homosexuals invite trouble and court hostility. The laws of the universe are very clear; what goes around comes around. What you send out comes back to you. Terrance, Antwan, Hank, Laverne and Joe(not yet deceased) provoked trouble, caused drama and invented enemies were there were none. How did they expect their lives to end? Honestly, I believe they probably didn't care.

The ratio of homosexual men murdered was found to be 50 times that of the general population. Other causes of death include substance abuse and suicide.
Studies show homosexuals have a greater risk of suffering from a psychiatric problem then heterosexuals. These problems include anti-social personality disorder, bulimia, paranoia and depression.

In 1973, after intense pressure from homosexuals and their advocates, The American Psychiatric Association removed homosexuality from its list of mental disorders. Because of this reversal homosexuals were able to boast they were as normal as heterosexuals and fought any and all scientific research that even suggested psychiatric problems. But it wasn't until 1992 that homosexuality was taken out of the psychiatric manual used by most other nations.

Keeping the above facts in mind lets examine all the scientific research homosexuals don't want you to know about. The Riess Study (1980) found that homosexuals showed definite "personal and emotional oversensitivity." The Remafdei et al Study (1998) found suicide attempts among homosexuals were six times greater then the average heterosexual. In The Archives of General Psychiatry; Fergusson (1999), Herrell (1999), Sandfort (2001) and Bailey (1999) all concluded that homosexual people are at substantially higher risk for some forms of emotional problems, including suicide, major depression, anxiety disorder, conduct disorder and nicotine dependence.

The Fergusson Study (1999) followed a large New Zealand group from birth to their twenties. The study showed a significantly higher occurrence of depression, anxiety disorder, substance abuse, and thoughts about suicide amongst those who were homosexually active. –N.E. Whitehead PhD

Studies from Anon (1995), Saphira and Glover (2000), and Welch (2000) show lesbians are about twice as likely to have sought help for mental problems as heterosexual women but only about 35% of them over their lifespan did. Saghir and Robins (1978) noted that when it comes to homosexuals and early death rates relationship breakups motivate suicide attempts, not outside pressures from society. They also noted the homosexuals inability to accept ones self. That's not at all a surprise sense homosexuality is not a natural human state.

"Suicide attempts are about three times higher for homosexuals then the rest of the population. Since homosexuals have greater numbers of partners and breakups, compared with heterosexuals, and sense long term gay male relationships are rarely monogamous, it is hardly surprising if suicide attempts are proportionally greater. The medium number of partners for homosexuals is four times higher then for heterosexuals." N.E. Whitehead, PhD -Whitehead and Whitehead study.

A study done in the Netherlands found a great amount of mental illness in homosexual people. That's important since the Netherlands has more tolerance for homosexuals then any other country on earth. In New Zealand, another country with great homosexual tolerance, suicide attempts are commensurate with the "homophobic" United States; another interesting fact. However, the Ross Study (1988) found that greater hostility towards homosexuals in the United States didn't result in higher levels of psychiatric problems then Denmark or the Netherlands.

In 2008 the Massachusetts Department of Public Health noted health disparities based on sexual orientation. People who identified themselves as homo or bi, suffered significantly higher incidences of depression, anxiety, illicit drug use, intimate partner violence, binge drinking, obesity, etc. It stated lesbians were 2.2 times more likely then heterosexual women to be obese. And this was in Massachusetts of all places.

Is bulimia a mental disorder? I've always read that it was. Carlat (1997) noted that 43% of bulimic males were homosexual or so called bisexual. That's 15 times that of the general population and is likely due to the obsession homosexual males have with appearance and physique. When it comes to homosexual behavior damage to the body and mind is rarely discussed. How does this 300lb. guerilla in the room continue to go unnoticed?

"When it comes to AIDS and protecting themselves it should be considered mentally disturbed to risk loosing one's life for sexual liberation. This is surely among the most extreme risks practiced by any significant fraction of society. I have not found a higher risk of death accepted by any similar –sized population."

- N.E. Whitehead, PhD

Let me break it down for you. If ten homosexuals were in a room and five of them had AIDS, four of them would still be willing to have unprotected sex with some of the people in that room. If I was in a room with ten women and I knew just one of them had A.I.D.S, but I didn't know which one, I wouldn't have sex with any of them. I'd simply leave the room. Get it! I would be crazy to do otherwise. By contrast homosexuals would still be lined up to get into that room. Is this not mentally disturbed behavior?

Who you with?

Who are your friends? By pointing them out you're looking at yourself. Like it or not, you become like those with whom you closely associate.-for better or worse. Someone told me 'the less you involve yourself with certain people the more your life will get better'. Take a look at people who are doing well. They don't tolerate or associate with negative thinking people. Negativity breeds negativity. Some of your so called friends don't want you to grow-because you may outgrow them. They shrewdly try to keep you from rising because you may rise above them-spiritually and financially; they'll no longer be able to control your heart or your wallet. *Are they really your friends?* Friends that don't help you soar will sit back and watch as you fall.

Stupidity is contagious. If your friends are self-starting go-getters they will strengthen your fortitude. If your friends are unproductive, and live their lives based on one excuse after another, you can become like them; a poor excuse who never lived up to your potential. Recognize a friend from someone who's there to hinder your growth. No matter what, take responsibility for your own actions. They may have been the bad influence, but the choice was yours. Learn from it. Move forward; stronger and wiser. **The worst feeling in the world is looking back at your life and asking; "what if."**

Don't let rain, sleet, hail, snow, children, drugs, jail, relationships or evil intentions break your spirit. Sometimes you have to beat the bushes to see where the snakes are hiding. You can't choose your family but you can choose your friends. Your family can be your friends- and friends can be like family. But you must choose wisely. Reach for your goals and your dreams will be there waiting. **Remember, God, nature and the universe are one**, and we were created with the very same elements. Therefore, 'god' is in us. This must be accepted and respected. Churches and religions come and go, but spirituality is the key to life itself. **And if God is in you, you will not fail!**

REFERENCES

Homosexuality and the Effeminization of Afrikan Males
- Mwalimu K. Bomani Baruti (Akoben House, 2003)

The Death of Black America-Eran Reya (Author House, 2007)

Slavery by Another Name: The Re-enslavement of Black Americans
From the Civil War to WW ll-Douglass A. Blackmon (Doubleday, 2008)

The New World Order-Ralph Epperson (Publius Press, 1990)

The Mind of Adolph Hitler-Walter Langer (Basic Books, 1972)

Dirt-Terrence McLaughlin (NY Dorsett Press, 1971)

Same Sex Unions in Pre-Modern Europe-John Boswell(New York: Villard, 1994)

The Destruction of Black Civilization: Great Issues of Race Between
4500 B.C. and 2000 A.D. (Third World Press, 1987)

God Is Not Great; How Religion Poisons Everything-Christopher Hitchens
(Twelve Books 2007)

After the Ball: How America Will Conquer Its Fear and Hatred of Gay in the 90's
-Hunter Madsen & Marshall Kirk (Plume 1990)

The Vagina monologues, 10th Anniversary Edition-Eve Ensler
(Random House)

Alternatives Magazine Issue 15

Reparative Therapy of Male Homosexuality-Joseph Nicolosi, Ph.D.
(Jason Aronson, Inc. 1997)